Edited by Angus Carlyle & Cathy Lane

On Listening

Uniformbooks 2013

First published 2013
Reprinted 2015
Copyright © CRiSAP/individual contributors, 2013

ISBN 978-1-910010-01-3

Uniformbooks
7 Hillhead Terrace, Axminster, Devon EX13 5JL
www.uniformbooks.co.uk

Printed and bound by TJ International Ltd, Padstow, Cornwall

Contents

Listening Spaces

Listening Devices

Listening to Self and Other

On Listening

Listening has become an increasingly popular subject of study. It features in conferences, in academic journals, in doctoral research projects. However, reflexive listening is an applied practice that exceeds the boundaries of academic institutions to take its place in a number of everyday settings. This book aims to connect the scholarly and the experiential and extend the contemporary discourse on listening.

The essays that are curated here have been commissioned from authors whose work places them in a variety of settings: artists, activists, scholars, scientists. We are conscious that texts in other languages may hold valuable insights, and as editors producing a book in English we have sought international contributions and these lead us all beyond institutional and national categories to listening worlds of expansive horizons.

The book has been organised into four primary sections: Listening Perspectives, Listening Spaces, Listening Devices and Listening to Self and Other. This structure represents one of many possible approaches to the material and through it our intention has been to reveal commonalities rather than expose differences, make connections across disciplines, across geographical locations and across methodologies. In some of the essays, listening is the necessarily primary mode of apprehension—for the musician, for the radio audience, the collector of folk-songs, for the sound recordist. In others, the listening practice provides a new way to understand or describe a situation or interaction—crowds in an urban square, private space in the Renaissance city, the world beyond the prisoner's hood, the temple garden in Kyoto.

The practice of listening can operate to reveal a parallel reality —one that lies below, beyond, behind or inside that which is imme-diately accessible. While listening may not always capture the 'objective' scene in an instant, the essentially immersive nature of the listening experience over time can lead to a meditative, inward-looking introspection, disappearing as soon as it is grasped. Conversely, that very immersion can place the listener at the centre of things, offering an intimate connection to place and its inhabitants, sacred and profane.

On Listening builds on the considerable contributions made by composers and musicians including John Cage, Pierre Schaeffer, R. Murray Schafer and Pauline Oliveros; on the theoretical writings of Don Ihde and Jean-Luc Nancy; and on the more recent books *Listening to Noise and Silence* and *Sinister Resonance* by our colleagues Salomé Voegelin and David Toop. Given the fundamental importance of listening not just in an artistic context but throughout lived experience, we also recognise that there is yet to be a publication that takes a wide-ranging, multidisciplinary perspective on listening as an applied practice. This publication aims to begin that process.

Angus Carlyle & Cathy Lane
London, November 2013

Angus Carlyle is a co-director at CRiSAP at the University of the Arts, London. He is curious about how we understand our environment, through sound and through our other senses. He edited the book *Autumn Leaves* for Double Entendre (2007), made the sound work '51° 32' 6.954" N / 0° 00' 47.0808" W' for the 'Sound Proof' group show (2008), co-curated the exhibition 'Sound Escapes' at Space Gallery in London (2009) and produced the CD *Some Memories of Bamboo* (2009) for the label Gruenrekorder. In 2012 he completed a sixth-month residency project called 'Viso Come Territorio' / 'Face As Territory', a collaboration with seven photographers based around a village on a Southern Italian hillside. Another work, *Air Pressure*, has been a collaboration with anthropologist Rupert Cox which led to an exhibition (part of the Asia Triennial Manchester), a CD/booklet and two films.

Cathy Lane is a composer, sound artist, lecturer and researcher. She is interested in how sound relates to the past, our histories, our environment and our collective and individual memories. Her current areas of creative and theoretical engagement are with spoken word composition, field recording, sound and gender, and, of course, listening. Other publications include *Playing with Words: The Spoken Word in Artistic Practice*, an anthology of works from over forty leading contemporary sound artists and composers who use words as their material and inspiration. Her forthcoming CD, *The Hebrides Suite*, a series of compositions that explore history and memory related to the Outer Hebrides, remote islands off the West coast of Scotland, will be released by Gruenrekorder in late 2013. Cathy Lane established the department of Sound Arts and Design and now co-directs Creative Research in Sound Arts Practice (CRiSAP) at the University of the Arts, London.

Introduction by Angus Carlyle

Listening Perspectives

Perhaps there is no listening perspective as such. Michel Chion, for one, cautions us that the long-established cinematic convention of the Point of View (POV) cannot be readily translated into the sonic equivalent of a point of audition.

In part, this is explained by the radical sensorial openness through which our ears, body, auditory cortex and relevant parts of the mind-brain encounter the heard. We are back with McLuhan here and his emblematic physiology of "no earlids"; rather than the flat, angled, and planar focus of the eyes, our ears are continually, radially, alert —even during sleep—to the sounds that surround. This distinction begins early. The eyes are said to only begin their operation during the peri-natal passage and at first present the infant with a world of depthless gradations of grey. By the time colour and distance swim into view, in the days after birth, the ears would normally have already been receiving stimulus for five months. Perhaps the foetal soundscape exhibits that broadband shimmer that "contains all the sounds and none of them at the same time" which Francisco López raises to an almost cosmological principle in his essay 'Wine and dust'?

And it is these sounds which are the other part of the explanation, since they, too, conspire to problematise any single discrete point of audition. Rather than the discernible scene revealed in optical perspective, the sheer dynamism of sound somehow eludes such capture. With solar light constantly bathing the planet, objects and structures possess a reflected solidity. It is different with sound, as Peter Cusack reminds us in his beautiful interpretation of Mazen Kerbaj's *Starry Night.* "Suddenly an explosion shatters the stillness. The sound instantly lights up the city as it reverberates off buildings and hillsides briefly revealing the panorama, as would a lightning flash. Simultaneously, the blast triggers car alarms and sets dogs barking, pin-pointing their positions near and far before they fade to a tense quiet waiting for the next bomb to fall."

Cusack's adumbration of a sonic journalism is one of the perspectives on listening assembled here that locates itself in a universe replete with potential meaning. He shares with Ultra-red a sense that to listen to what is there or, as this activist-artist collective significantly claim, *"to listen for what is left out and why"*, is to orientate oneself towards the truth. The Protocols that Ultra-red have developed "seek to put the recording and its listeners into process by privileging the ear that hears over the sound recording itself". Conversely, Michael Gallagher, through an extended commentary on a number of resonant examples, problematises the assumption that listening is primarily concerned with the transmission of either truth or meaning and even that it is an inherently positive activity, inviting us to consider instead "questions about what listening *does*".

The ambivalence that Gallagher pours into the field of listening, wells up in other essays here. It resurfaces in Sarha Moore's ethnomusicological account of the flat second, a musical note which is variously attributed the status of the "normal", of "intense pathos", of "the bottled grief of the male", of "spiritual bliss", one that to still others represents the "doomy", the "dark" and the "relaxing". This ambivalence springs up again for David Toop, in his claim that to adopt a listening attitude is to recruit the ostensibly mute and the inert into vital, "listenable" participation in sensory life. There is ambivalence, too, in Moushumi Bhowmik and Sukanta Majumdar's evocative contribution where, amongst other things, listening to an audio recording can simultaneously pull closer and push further away.

Mark Peter Wright and Rupert Cox arrive at a similar destination from very distant points of departure, each travelling by very different means. Cox unearths the treasures of Japanese Zen to discover that the anthropologist lying on the gravel path is "listening to their own listening". Wright's photographs of different terrain, some bearing the recent impressions of human feet, are accompanied by what almost amounts to a *kôan* suggesting a parallel suspicion that the ultimate and inescapable subject of listening may be the listener's listening itself.

In this section and throughout *On Listening* as a whole, listening becomes active; indeed listening becomes creative. As López has it, lying on the wet rain forest floor rather than the temple path, "I feel like a creator; not because I am recording or because I might be later 'composing' something with these sounds, but simply because I am listening... with dedication and passion".

The pictures are spread before us like disjointed tiles—photographs from our long and entwined journey through music in Bengal. It's two of us; one singer and writer, the other sound recordist and sound artist. We have been travelling together, sometimes also with friends, in this eastern part of the Indian subcontinent for almost a decade, recording music that comes out of people's lives; in sound, image and text.

Moushimi Bhowmik & Sukanta Majumdar

Images of Listening: Word-Pictures from a Journey Through Music

On a cold and dry afternoon in January 2005, Golam Shah Fokir was playing music in his house in Shaspur village in Birbhum and we were recording him. "Take what you can", he said to the camera, "these might well be the last pictures". Also the last songs, as it turned out within a couple of months of our field trip.

Golam Shah Fokir used to sing songs about the mysteries of the universe and the divine experience of love—they are called *fokiri* and *murshidi gaan*. For decades he had sung in shrines and festivals, gathering communities of listeners around him. The singer is also the teacher, imparting lessons to those who listen in faith, the insiders. Our presence was for a different purpose, hence our listening was also different; we knew Golam Shah would soon be gone and with him, a time in history. It is difficult to know how old he was then. Time can both weather, as well as make wiser. But Golam Shah seemed to have a premonition of death and

on this day he played it out almost with a sense of humour. Totally photogenic, he posed for the camera, singing, talking, instructing, smoking; conscious of all the attention he was drawing and the recording equipment that surrounded him in that passing moment. He knew the value of being recorded, he knew in his own way about the power of recordings to preserve time, for he kept instructing his sons Salam and Jamir to sing their best. We took pictures of him playing with his sons, alone with his old violin, with his wife, daughters, sons, their families, children, villagers, with his followers and friends and also with us. He had full sway over his domain that day, almost pushing his frail body, voice and breath beyond their limits. We captured his image as he listened to our recording of his songs; then returned the headphones satisfied, saying, "Khub high class!"

First there is the performance, the moment of the making of the music, which is also the moment of recording, as well as the moment of experiencing the music live; then follows the ritual of listening to the recording. Sometimes we have conversation with the players, then we too—mostly Moushumi—become players. Sukanta silently records. He passes around the headphones after the recording is over, some listen, others look on. Later we look at photographs of singers and audiences caught in the act of listening. Words emanate from the images—words, the sound of the words, word-pictures, evoking memory and desire.

There are different ways of listening and different expectations written on these varied faces. Chandrabati Mashima, who was about 78 when we first recorded her in her home in Sylhet town in 2006, had appeared totally self-conscious from the beginning. She would stop us in the middle of the song if she felt she had made a mistake. Erase that bit, she said to Sukanta. Then when she listened to the recording, it seemed as if she was intently examining her reflection in the mirror. A smile of contentment lit up her face from time to time.

At the other end of the spectrum, far from this personal response, would be an obscure village by the Surma river called Shadhusree, also in the Sylhet region, where both singer and audience had collectively made music all through a night in the spring of 2008. Such is the nature of this music—it is ritualistic and communal. At the break of dawn they listened together to their songs.

It is such an absorbing image! One listens, others watch, but somehow their faces are as animated, as if they can gauge the sound from the expression on the listener's face, who is actually listening alone, through the headphones. In our heads, their last song ushering in a new day, the *probhati* keeps playing, long after it is over. *Probhato samay kale, Shachiro angina majhe/ Gourchand nachiya beray re.* The mad poet sings and dances at dawn, touching his listeners with the spirit of love.

We talk about ourselves. Sometimes I think I miss the touch of the skin of the sound. My listening is mediated by the machine, filtered through the microphone, recorder and headphones. I also miss seeing all the things going on around me.

I feel inadequate in other ways. I am too focused on the immediate and obvious to hear anything else. Sometimes the visual distracts me. Often it is only in your recording that I hear the details. Think how Hajera Bibi of Faridpur was talking about another time in her life which was filled with people. She kept saying, my voice wasn't like this, this is no song that I am singing, remember?

Yes, the dog barked and there was the prayer call of nightfall in the distance. Isha'a. Someone was drawing water from the screeching hand pump in the courtyard. A child was crying, her grandniece's I think. Hajera Bibi was trying to recall names and words of songs.

I know. I've heard that fading light in your recording.

Sarha Moore

The Listener is the Artist [1]

> The gypsy came to realize that it was mainly the melodies with a Phrygian cadence which pleased the collector. From then onwards, whenever it was at all possible, he brought even the commonest melody to an end with a Phrygian cadence, while his companion obligingly observed the effect on the face of the listener.
> —Balint Sárosi *Gypsy Music*.[2]

On listening to the flat second:[3] by definition there is a first, a key-note, thus a relationship. As listeners we then create meaning.

We cannot know all the meanings given to a musical work by its creators and we may or may not care about this.

Is it possible to listen and enjoy in an ethical way with a desire, not to 'understand' the music but, to 'be here now'?

I'm an English musician from Croydon, putting my Croydon ear to the 'surprise', 'illegitimacy', 'orientalism', the 'exotic' sound of the flat second.

1. Molnár, A. 1937. *Magyar-e a cigányzene?* Budapest: a szerzo kiadása.
2. Sárosi, B. 1970. *Gypsy Music*. Budapest: Corvina Press, pp.245–246.
3. It is the pitch between Doh and Re in a scale, the Phrygian second.

Opposite & overleaf:
What do you hear? How do you hear this note differently?
Fill in the spaces in the table and let me know: http://phrygian2.blogspot.co.uk/
You can also find a dedicated page of links that relate to the subject of this essay at that blog address.

Sarha Moore:	Listening To Other Opinions and Thoughts:	
To me it's music from somewhere away from the familiar. It's the ultimate *Other*, the feeling had by everyone who doesn't fit in.	"For the West the flat second is quite an exotic thing. For us it's a normal thing, we just think of it as another *makam* [Turkish Classical 'scale'], we don't attribute feelings to them." Cahit Baylav, Turkish Classical Musician, London 2009	
It has an *emotional* tug bringing pathos, tears, but also pleasure. It is also the most gloriously alive pitch—unstable, driving, dissonant and full of un-ease.	"When you... know what is the cause of that emotional movement you think now ok... it's so interesting to see people react when you just change the second note... your body naturally goes with this second, you turn differently... all of a sudden your body moves, your ear, everything just turns to the different direction." Merima Ključo, Bosnian *sevda* accordionist, Amsterdam 2011	"*Sandhi Prakash* [dusk], as you will agree, is a very sensitive period... the pathos is very intense and therefore... this *komal re* [flat second] from the lower note is used for intense pathos... in the *Sandhi Prakash* period. However, the *komal re* in raga *Marva* [an Indian Classical 'scale'] is the bottled grief of the male." Arvind Parikh, Indian Classical Music Scholar, Mumbai 2011
It's thwarting the expectation of gravity: the ball caught just before reaching earth.	"It's always sad, but sad doesn't mean you've lost your purse, it means 'closer to God'." Rafaqat Ali Khan, Pakistani Qawwali singer, Lahore 2009	
It's lingering on the longing, delicious anticipation, deferred gratification. It's cool.	"In the dusk *komal re* is more prominent because it's relaxing... It's the end of the day, you're going to relax, chill out, the work's tension is finished, and your partner, your lover is coming, you want to relax, in front of the box maybe." Baluji Shrivastav, Indian Sitar player, London 2009	The *komal re* in raga Bhairav? "I'll have to sing it... This is kind of a delight. It's a delight of spiritual bliss. That's how I would like to describe it... We also tend to put something of our own personality into the *swara* [note]... it's a symbiotic thing between the *swara* and me... and the *swara* that you will see and feel is going to be different, I believe." Subroto Roy, Indian Classical Singer, Puna 2011

Sarha Moore:	Listening To Other Opinions and Thoughts:	
But it's also tense. The *tension* of being powerless and out of kilter with the norm.	"It's tight, like Israel." Firaz Nadaf, Palestinian Metal guitarist, Nazareth 2010	
Tension that can only be released by sinking: into depression, Hell? On listening to Heavy Metal, the strong, insistent sound makes me aware of the power of the release of anger, of the *transgressive* sound: dissonance at its greatest—'shock and awe'.	*Jaws* was the first time I heard it... [the] flat second makes it really 'doomy'... what a flat second does to you... on a human level. It creates the skull and the spiral to Hell." Pete Herbert, English Metal bassist, Dagenham, 2009	"The scale is definitely not happy: Arabic, Ali Baba and the 40 thieves. Flat second is associated with sinister, not necessarily threatening, but dark, not 'happy clappy'." Luke Raynor, English Metal guitarist, London, 2009
The power of the Other to induce fear and un-ease.	"I think a lot of people in Metal in the Western World play it because... it has that half-tone diabolic, bad boy kind of essence to it... quite dissonant to the ear... but for me it's really nothing about that. I don't try to be diabolic and to create any controversial sounds, or dissonance sounds in any way. For me [it] is far from dissonant." Yossi Sassi Sa-aron, Israeli Metal guitarist, Tel Aviv, 2010	"In the physical bodies [in the Western World] that are accustomed back to the 15th century it is going to sound profoundly alien, and there may be even a physical reaction... When you go to musics of North Africa and the Middle East you don't want that reaction. It's not appropriate. But you're listening to lots of other parameters at the same time that go together to create a reaction." Susan McClary, New Musicologist, Los Angeles, 2010
I'll never hear it in the same way again.		
Is it inappropriate for me to listen for it, to feel sad, to sigh? The embedded sedimented meanings are there, appropriate or not. How do I make an appropriate listening? How do I listen without prejudice?	"It's also how you perceive, *how you hear* it, how your nervous system reacts to it. But it definitely is dark, I think everyone can agree to that... Maybe if you walk around in the cities... like Damascus, like Cairo, ...older cities and more deep cities and you can probably hear why this note exists in this music... In my music though—don't listen for it." Boikutt, Palestinian Sound Artist, Ramallah, 2010	

Peter Cusack

Field Recording as Sonic Journalism

One of the most stunning field recordings of the past decade is *Starry Night* by Mazen Kerbaj. Mazen is Lebanese and lives in Beirut. He describes the recording as *"a minimalistic improvisation by: mazen kerbaj/trumpet, the israeli air force/bombs"*. It documents the sounds on the balcony of his flat on the night of 15/16th of July 2006 during Israel's summer war against Hezbollah in Lebanon. The recording starts with small breathy sounds made on the trumpet. They are quiet, but seem very close. One listens attentively. Suddenly an explosion shatters the stillness. The sound instantly lights up the city as it reverberates off buildings and hillsides briefly revealing the panorama, as would a lightning flash. Simultaneously, the blast triggers car alarms and sets dogs barking, pin-pointing their positions near and far before they fade to a tense quiet waiting for the next bomb to fall. It is one of those rare recordings where sound exhibits the same power of illumination as light. Throughout Mazen continues to play minimal trumpet, quietly creative against the violence. His recording not only documents the events taking place, but is an act of imaginative defiance in its own right. For a listener the impact is powerful. The perspective reveals the city's geography, a major aspect of its current political context and a very personal response to the situation. It is the dramatic conjunction of these elements within a single recording that makes it so memorable.

Of course, this is a unique recording made in wartime. Most recordists' subject matter is far more normal and everyday. But the power and layered elements of this recording vividly convey the situation. It is a graphic example of 'sonic-journalism', journalism of and for the ear—the sound equivalent of photo-journalism.

What is sonic-journalism? In radio news, current affairs and sound documentary—and indeed on TV despite the significance of images— the dominance of speech, whether as spoken reportage, interviews, commentary or discussion, is unquestioned. Sonic-journalism is based on the idea that all sound, including non-speech, gives information about places and events and that listening provides valuable insights different from, yet complementary to, visual images and language. This does not exclude speech but re-addresses the balance towards the relevance of other sounds. In practice, field recordings become the means to achieve this. Recordings can, of course, be used in many ways. In my view, sonic-journalism occurs when field recordings are allowed adequate space and time to be heard in their own right, when the focus is on their original factual and emotional content, and when they are valued for what they are rather than as source material for further work (as is often the case in sound art or music). Sonic-journalism can be specifically created or can refer to these qualities in recordings originally made for other purposes, such as *Starry Night*.

What do field recordings offer in this context? Most obviously they give basic information about places and events by virtue of the sounds, and their sources, that we identify. Language and visual images also give such information. Indeed, it is arguable they do so rather more explicitly than sound. The interpretation of sound certainly benefits from a knowledge of context in the same way that captions and titles enhance photographs. However, field recordings convey far more than basic facts. Spectacular or not, they also transmit a powerful sense of spatiality, atmosphere and timing. This applies even when the technical quality is poor. These factors are key to our perception of place and movement and so add substantially to our understanding of events and issues. They give a compelling impression of what it might actually be like to be there. Sound is our prime sense of all-around spatiality and listening gives us a point of ear. It enables us judge how far we are from the events and to ask how we might feel and react in the circumstances. Certainly, with recordings and broadcasts we know we are not there, but even at this reduced level there is a subjective engagement and intuitive understanding that, in my view, are field recordings' special strength. Such elements allow sonic-journalism a significant impact that is qualitatively different from visual images or language.

Of course the news media already makes use of field recordings (probably referred to as location recordings). Indeed there has been a noticeable increase recently, particularly on BBC radio. But it is almost always as a 'sound effect'—a burst of gunfire from Afghanistan, a snatch of national anthem on a royal visit, a line of protest song in an Arab square (all heard BBC Radio 4/World Service, 17th May 2011). They add a touch of actuality, but rarely last more than a few seconds before being faded down for the ever dominant speaking voice. Field recording's power of atmosphere, spatiality and timing are hardly acknowledged. This is a pity, as crews sent to news hot spots are uniquely placed to capture such material and it is our loss that they are so rarely broadcast. Very occasionally, though, one does get through. An especially poignant example occurs 18 minutes into Jon Snow's 'Tsunami Diary' from Japan, 16th March 2011 (C4 TV). Amid the tsunami wreckage, amazingly, one loudspeaker from a devastated town's public address system still works. It is playing the 5pm music that marks the end of the school day. Despite the blandest of electronic arrangements the tune is easily recognisable. It is *Yesterday*—Paul McCartney's best known song of lost love and shattered dreams—here a quite surreal, and moving, comment on the destruction we see before us. Sound art, as well as sonic-journalism, can learn from this clip.

These examples are sonic-journalism for the listener. Equally important are the advantages for investigators. Sounds are very potent triggers for research. Attentive listening on location can reveal sonic threads running through the narratives and issues under examination and suggest unexpected questions and directions to be pursued.

In May 2006 I visited Chernobyl. It was a field trip for the project 'Sounds from Dangerous Places', which explores what insights sound can offer into the ecological, social and political contexts of places of major environmental damage. My first recording inside the exclusion zone was a surprise. Our driver had stopped for a cigarette and immediately I heard the fizz and pop of electricity. We had parked beside a pylon and above us the cables were crackling with use. A chaffinch sang nearby and wind blew through the pines. It was an ear-catching combination so I switched on the recorder. However the sound raised a question. All Chernobyl's reactors had shut down so where was this electricity coming from and what was it for? Later our guide explained that Chernobyl still requires large amounts of power to maintain the reactors even in their shut down state, to continue the unfinished clean-up operations and to support the thousands of people who continue to live and work in the zone. The sound recorded was electricity flowing in the wrong direction, into Chernobyl rather than out, a sonic manifestation of the massive drain on Ukraine's resources that Chernobyl has become.

Further research led to more information about Chernobyl's never-ending clean-up and, more widely, on what happens when a nuclear reactor's lifespan ends. A reactor cannot just be switched off. Even if decommissioned without incident and the nuclear core removed, decades must pass before the buildings and immediate area are radiologically safe. Maintenance and security are essential for the entire period. Chernobyl's exploded Reactor 4 cannot be decommissioned. What remains of the melted core lies under tons of aging and cracking concrete. Repairs are constant and a long-term solution is increasingly urgent. A massive new containment structure has been proposed, but international arguments over the huge cost are unresolved. Researching this has taken time but hearing that unexpected fizz of electricity was the essential start. It is still a key memory when I'm reminded of these issues. Following sonic threads became a particularly effective research method at Chernobyl. Another led to the significance of the region's rich folklore in trying to appreciate the disaster's impact on rural people—the vast majority of those affected.

Postscript

As I write—April/May 2011, Chernobyl's 25th anniversary—the latest nuclear disaster is unfolding at Fukushima, Japan. Nobody knows how it will turn out, but the reactors no longer produce electricity. Like at Chernobyl, there will now be Japanese pylons crackling as electricity flows the wrong way into the stricken Fukushima plant rather than away from it.

The arguments for the recognition of sonic-journalism as a specific discipline are not intended to downplay any other medium. Far from it. Our senses and the media that address them cover different areas of perception. We gain a much fuller picture when they are in proper balance. Sound on its own is as incomplete as visual images and language on their own. Sonic-journalism makes the case for sound to contribute on an equal basis and to its strengths. How and in what forms might this happen? Mainstream radio and TV will probably be slow to innovate in this area. They anyway may not be the best means, as, aside from their own inertia, we, the audience, are equally fixed in our interpretation of them. For me the new possibilities are likely to come from new and mobile media, particularly as they bring potentially relevant technologies into contention such as GPS, mapping, instant communications and the ability to experience virtual and real space simultaneously.

Selected references

Starry Night, Mazen Kerbaj http://mazenkerblog.blogspot.com

Tsunami Diary, Jon Snow, C4 16 March 2011 *http://blogs.channel4.com/snowblog/days-japan-loss-invisible-threat/14875*. Many thanks to David Toop for drawing this to my attention.

Sounds from Dangerous Places, Peter Cusack, CD/Booklet ReR Records (ReR PC3&4)

Field recordist Chris di Laurenti http://www.delaurenti.net/ has regularly covered news events from a sonic perspective, for example *Live in New York at the Republican National Convention Protest 2 September–28 August 2004* and *N30: Live at the WTO*.

/ PROTOCOLS FOR A LISTENING SESSION / have been composed by Ultra-red for organizing collective listening to pre-recorded sounds. The protocols seek to put the recording and its listeners into process by privileging the ear that hears over the sound recording itself. [Glasgow, 90 min, 16. 05. 2010]

STEP A: Listen to sound recordings

0

1   *Introductions* — To begin; invite everyone in the group to introduce herself or himself by name, any organisational affiliation and the kind of work that they do. Participants can also say what they want to hear the group talk about.

2   *Listen to the sound recordings* — Play each recording one at a time over the sound-system without introduction. The sound recordings are of a previous event and prepared in advance for the purposes of generating dialogue

3   *"What did you hear?"* — After playing each sound recording, give the group two minutes to respond to the question, "What did you hear?" The group remains silent while everyone writes their responses on paper.

4   *Repeat steps #2 and #3 for each sound recording.*

STEP B: Identify theme or themes

1   *Report what you heard* — Compare all the responses to the sound recordings in the group. Note the responses that are convergent or similar and, especially, those that are divergent or different.

2   *Discuss the theme(s)* — After going around the group, discuss the most urgent issues to emerge from the responses to the sound recordings. The tendency in such discussions can be to arrive at an agreement on the important themes. The process of agreement often attempts to resolve differences in experience or knowledge. Give attention to those divergences, not as differences to be conquered or argued but as problems to be investigated.

3   *Determine the theme(s)* — Write down key themes that name the differences, and even contradictions, that arose from the discussion

4   *Write the theme(s)* — Rewrite the theme in the form of a question or a proposition that can be investigated in actual lived experiences, either one's own or in those communities where the theme organises the experience of everyday life.

Notes on the Protocols for a Listening Session (Glasgow Variation)

In composing the listening session protocols for Glasgow, Ultra-red members Chris Jones, Elliot Perkins and Dont Rhine introduced a number of alterations to the procedure that the collective had been using since the summer of 2009. The changes came about largely in response to the partnership with a local Glasgow collective, Strickland Distribution, comprising writers, researchers, artists and academics loosely grouped around Glasgow's *Variant* magazine.

The first chapter we would undertake together would be a walk through Glasgow's massively gentrified Merchant City district. The walk was led by Neil Gray from Strickland Distribution but often taken over by others with spontaneous bursts of group discussion at and between the various sites. Ultra-red followed, listened and recorded. A few other participants also made sound recordings that would be useful later on. The walk, entitled 'In the Shadow of Shadow' would feed into a second event the following weekend; a listening session held at the community-run Kinning Park Complex. In the interim, a series of strategy meetings ensued between Ultra-red and Strickland in quiet nooks tucked within lively working class pubs. These discussions informed a decision to experiment with our usual listening procedure. First, instead of using sound objects drawn from Ultra-red's existing archive we would play recordings taken from the walk that involved many of the same people attending the listening session. Second, we recruited local activists for small group facilitation. Third, we stressed a definition of themes based on divergences. And, fourth, we proposed as an outcome the formation of investigation teams. These changes proved enormously productive in what we learned, even where the actual execution fell short of the hoped-for effect.

We want to acknowledge that this listening session followed over a year of multiple visits to Glasgow. These visits demonstrated Ultra-red's interest in the city and helped to initiate a shift in the nature of the invitation from that of an arts context to a more activist context. At the time of this writing, that shift is by no means resolved. 'In the Shadow of Shadow' marks the beginning. It is important to acknowledge the tremendous commitment of our sponsor, the Scottish arts organization, Arika. While 'In the Shadow of Shadow' occurred as part of their experimental music festival, Uninstal, Arika gave the project the autonomy it needed to develop organically and continues to support the process beyond Ultra-red's involvement.

A year on from our work with Strickland Distribution we still maintain contact with Neil Gray. That contact is largely the result of our shared investments in housing and gentrification struggles. Ultra-red's work with migrant constituencies in Glasgow invariably brings Neil and ourselves to the same places. One year after writing the above dispatch (itself written a few weeks after the events it describes), we have received updates from Neil as well as Barry and Bryony from Arika who continue to support the work of what has come to be known as the Right to the City Forum (RTTC). To our great satisfaction, they all report that the protocols drafted for the Kinning Park event continue to play a major role in structuring subsequent RTTC meetings.

Whilst it would be truthful to say there was a degree of disappointment amongst ourselves as we learned that the sound component had been dropped from the protocols, it would seem that they have proven to be useful within RTTC. It was not long before other groups would take on facilitating RTTC, most notably the Burgh Angel group who produce a community activist newspaper in Glasgow's Maryhill area. In subsequent uses of the protocols, sound recordings have been replaced with newspaper articles or text composed by RTTC members. Others who have in some way participated in or contributed to the Forum have taken the protocols into other spaces and practices. Local activists used the protocols again as a basis for some of the initial meetings of Glasgow Against Education Cuts in early 2011. In each instance, alterations to the original protocols suggest some of the ways others make use of the guidelines and adjust them to their own political situation.

Those of us in Ultra-red take much encouragement from the fact that the protocols continue to circulate. At the same time, we have also noted that they have made their way into more dubious uses. Recently we received an invitation to attend a group critique of a PhD art exhibition in Glasgow. Much to our surprise, the students had chosen to structure the critique around the 'Shadow of Shadow' protocols. Whilst this was an attempt to engage critically with a piece of artwork, this seemed to be the only loose investment of all of those in attendance. The actual practice of criticality had nothing to do with a politically-motivated collective inquiry. What became devoid of sound with the RTTC use of the protocols had become devoid of political stakes in the context of a conventional academy art critique. We know from history and the machinery of dialectics that appropriation is inevitable. Practices and processes born in political struggle become co-opted to purposes for which they are perhaps ill-suited. The useful question when confronted with such a recuperation is not to ask *what* is co-opted but *to listen for what is left out and why*?

Exchanges

To remain in one place, over duration and listen.   22.05.10

What is imposed?   12.06.10

What is lost?   12.02.12

What remains?   18.08.10

David Toop

It Is Nothing

faint sound of something in its beginning

In March 2009 I was invited to give a lecture and solo performance at the GRM Festival 'Présences Electroniques' in Paris. During my free time I visited the Musée Picasso and found my ideas on the history of listening shifting as I viewed a remarkable sequence of paintings and relief constructions depicting musical instruments, particularly guitars.

My notebook from the time records mounting puzzlement and excitement whereby the mystery of Picasso dwelling so insistently on guitars and violins was shadowed by close thoughts on the representation of spatiality, captured time and auditory events in an otherwise flat, static and silent medium. At that point I had completed (or so I thought) the writing of my book, *Sinister Resonance*, in which I explore the potentiality of a silent medium—painting for example—as auditory device. A compulsion to write the book came from frustration with the self-limiting discourse of what we know as sound art, a repetitive, centripetal parading of 'heroes' whose predictability served to solidify an otherwise fluid practice.

Perhaps the implausibility of considering Picasso as a node of anti-history, even a primordial flash that ignited sound work in the 20th century, is an encouragement to consider the proposition seriously. I made notes on the relief constructions Picasso made in 1926, the materials a mix of ropes, newsprint, hessian, nails, string, a spring, tacks and canvas, all of them named *Guitar*: "The first of these menaces, sound hole torn out of sacking, nails protruding point-out; the second more like the soft imprint of the thought of a guitar pressed into sand, though the tension of the strap suggests a drawn bow string in both." Of *Mandolin and Clarinet*, from 1913, I wrote: "In this one, the instruments are exploded, as if their inner resonance has been turned inside out."

faint sound of no outside, no inside

A music is implicit. They are listenable, these paintings and constructions. They raise a question that only becomes greater when cubism is considered as a whole: the obsessional returning to musical instrument as still life in Picasso, Georges Braque and Juan Gris. This fixation with sonic technology is unavoidable; any history of cubism will pass a mystified remark before moving on to more settled issues. With an increasing focus on the significance of the object, notably in MoMA's exhibition—*Picasso Guitars 1912-1914*—the question is examined more thoroughly. "Picasso did not play an instrument and is said to have had no patience with most types of music," writes Anne Umland in the MoMA catalogue.[1] She considers the attraction of guitar music to Picasso—"its associations with café life and with flamenco music, a contradictory genre both primitive and modern, Spanish and gypsy, fixed and improvisational…"[2] before concluding that his decision to construct a guitar in 1912 was "an act that allowed him to discover what, specifically, the guitar had to offer him as a structure, or model, for a particular form of contained spatiality and for a particular vocabulary of simple, separable, iconic signs."[3]

Both of these points resonate. Lewis Kachur examines Picasso's fabled indifference to music more closely and finds a rather different story, in which his tastes (as we might expect from a painter whose vision was so forceful) ran to direct expression: the rough sound of a Catalan folk shawm called the tenora, or, at the other end of an imagined scale of refinement, the compositions of Erik Satie (a master of deceptive simplicity) and Déodat de Séverac. As an aside, Kachur draws a parallel: the embedded signs ubiquitous in cubism—the motif of the musical instrument, the scraps of newspaper and sheet music—and the strategy common to composers of the period in which folk tunes, popular songs from the music hall and cabaret and American ragtime and jazz were collaged, in the sense of being also embedded within the flow of a score.[4]

faint sound of faint sounding no sound

"Do you know how to clean sounds?" Satie wrote in 1913. "It's a filthy business."[5] His ironic wit applies itself to the notion of sonic materiality, just as Picasso's wit applied itself to the dismemberment

1. Umland, Anne. 2011. *Picasso Guitars 1912-1914*. New York: The Museum of Modern Art. p.20.
2. ibid, p.21.
3. ibid, p.22.
4. Kachur, Lewis. 'Picasso, popular music and collage Cubism (1911-12)'. *The Burlington Magazine*, vol.135, No.1081, Apr. 1993. p.256.
5. Satie, Erik, quoted in Perloff, Nancy. 1993. *Art and the Everyday: Popular Entertainment and the Circle of Erik Satie*. Oxford: Clarendon Press. p.83.

of forms. The void of the guitar, its volume out of which issues volume, disgorges itself. The vessel of sound is opened up, emptied out and that which is nothing becomes solid. His cardboard *Guitar* of 1913 has been variously described as "a new sculptural language", and "a crucial rupture in modern art's history". As for Picasso, his reaction was a shrug: "It's nothing, it's *el guitare!*", his insouciance echoed and amplified by André Salmon: "The watertight compartments are demolished. We are delivered from painting and sculpture, which have already been liberated from the tyranny of genres. It is neither this nor that. It is nothing. It's *el guitare!*"[6]

Alongside the stencilled image of a bottle of Anis del Mono, the *Guitar* of 1913 sat on a table, partial and flimsy but nonetheless 'real', all suspended in space in front of two overlapped sheets of wallpaper. Also in 1913, Picasso made the more complex *Construction with Guitar Player and Violin*, a work existing only in studio photographs of the time in which a real guitar was suspended from a 'wall' on which was drawn the outline of a guitar player. An arm with hand, made from newspaper, stretched down from the outlined guitarist to the floating guitar. Hanging on the wall is the paper violin from 1913 and set in front is a café table with wine bottle, pipe and cup. There is nothing in the piece that is sound in itself, no sound in the process of becoming, and yet we can listen. "Art should not be a *trompe l'oeil*, but a *trompe l'esprit*," said Picasso.[7] The eye is not deceived; nor is the ear. There is nothing, yet the mind is hearing.

6. Quoted in Umland, Anne, op cit., p.27.
7. Reference in Markus, Ruth. 'Picasso's Guitar, 1912: The Transition from Analytical to Synthetic Cubism'. *Assaph, Studies in Art History* 2. Tel Aviv University. 1996. p.238.

Michael Gallagher

Listening, Meaning and Power

In 2011, the UK government embarked upon a 'listening exercise' to consult with the public on a controversial policy to reform the National Health Service. This came following widespread criticism of the policy, which was seen by many as an attempt to further privatise and marketise the service. The Health Secretary claimed that the government wanted to "pause, listen, reflect and improve" their plans, and that the listening exercise was "an opportunity for people to share their views and have their voices heard" (Department of Health, 2011). In response, some critics argued that the listening exercise would be a smokescreen, a charade to appease voters and lend false legitimacy to a course of action that had already been decided upon, rather than a genuine attempt to engage with the public.

This is one instance of a common discourse about listening. On the one hand, an idealistic view is offered, which suggests that the hopes and dreams of democracy can be realised if the 'powers that be' will listen to the voices of those who have hitherto been ignored, silenced and excluded. On the other hand, it is invariably argued that such attempts to listen are often tokenistic, cynical tactics which promise much but rarely result in any meaningful change. This oppositional schema of 'genuine' versus 'tokenistic' listening can easily be applied to all kinds of initiatives: youth parliaments and community councils; participatory and action research; the plethora of feedback question-naires that now populate the spaces of retail and public services; the ubiquitous "how's my driving?" stickers on commercial vehicles.

This discourse about listening hinges on two assumptions that I want to call into question.

The first assumption is that listening is primarily about the transmission of meaning. The listener, be it a person, an audience or an organisation, is understood to be engaged in the act of comprehending what the other party is trying to express—their opinions, feelings, experiences, needs or desires. This kind of listening envisages 'voices' as conscious, intentional, coherent, articulate. Admittedly, a whole raft of social science methods has been developed to extend listening to those people—young children, disabled people, those from non-western cultures—who are less orally and aurally fixated. Non-verbal modes of communication such as drawing, photography, dance, drama and music are now included within the gamut of qualitative research (e.g. Veale, 2005). Yet in most cases the focus on communicated meaning remains. For example, research participants may be invited to draw or photograph their experiences, but this is usually follo-wed by a verbal elicitation of what the resulting images mean (e.g. Harper, 2002). In the performing arts and music, a similar paradigm persists, at least in the popular sphere. The audience is commonly understood to be listening to the various emotions, ideas and narratives that the performer, composer or songwriter is trying to express. All of this is summed up neatly by Blesser and Salter's definition of listening as "active attention or reaction to the meaning, emotions and symbolism contained within sound" (2007: 5).

I would argue that much of sound art and experimental music confronts this conception of listening with an alternative notion: maybe sound doesn't have to mean anything. Maybe meaning is as much something we bring to sound as something sound brings to us. Daniel describes this as "the territorialising force of human language and human knowledge upon the raw, inhuman fact of sound as a vibrational force" (2011: 45). Yet so often sound slips away, ambigu-ous, uncertain, unverifiable, elusive (Toop, 2010). I can understand the words you said to me, but what did the slight tremor in your voice mean? Was the pause in the middle of the sentence significant? Where is your accent from? If listening is about making rather than receiving meaning, then that process will always be compromised, messy, provisional and unfinished, taking place amidst a motley assemblage of sounding bodies, materials and spaces. It is a matter of negotiating some brief consensus amongst these various elements, building snippets of sense from a clutter of auditory signifiers which, like Lego bricks, can easily be pulled apart again and rearranged.

But there is also a kind of listening in which meaning plays an even more marginal role, and perhaps no role at all. In a conversation with a loved one on the telephone, for me the value lies as much in hearing a rendition of the person's voice as it does on comprehending what they have to say. Indeed, what they have to say may be entirely inconsequential, and yet the experience still feels important. It is about the connection: another being is vibrating, setting off a chain reaction of vibrations that is (literally) moving my body. The blackbird singing outside my window may be trying to communicate something, or he may not; I have no way of knowing for sure, but either way it makes no difference to my pleasure on hearing his song. Likewise when my neighbours play loud music, what the music means, where it is coming from, who wrote the song, who is playing it—at the most fundamental level, all of this is irrelevant. The fact is that on listening to it I am annoyed. This is the affective dimension of listening. In contrast to acousmatic listening, where a deliberate attempt is made to strip out all context in pursuit of a purely aesthetic experience, affective listening requires no such rarefications. It does not depend upon meaning, but neither does it need to purge it. It is listening in its most simple, everyday form, and perhaps its most vital.

The second assumption I wish to question is that listening, when done 'genuinely' and not 'tokenistically', is a good thing. From Cage to counselling to consultation, we are told that listening is essentially liberatory, that if there were more listening then the world would be a better place. Such notions overlook the fact that listening can be used for a wide variety of purposes. This is the case even (and perhaps especially) where listening is deep, careful, attentive and responsive. The phone hacking scandal that engulfed News International in 2011, for example, appears to have resulted from skilful acts of listening in which commercial motives had eclipsed ethical concerns.

If sound enacts power (Attali, 1985; Goodman, 2009), then so must listening. And as a technology of power, listening can be used tactically and strategically: to question musical conventions, as in 4'33" (LaBelle, 2006); in the production and re-formation of the self, as in psychotherapy and religious confession; for disciplinary purposes, as in court hearings and the interrogation of suspects; for surveillance, from practices of eavesdropping and espionage (Zbikowski, 2002) to audio recording for CCTV (Smeaton and McHugh, 2006) and crime-detection systems that listen for gunfire (Benjamin, 2002), to more mundane forms of regulation, such as controlling noise in libraries or schools (Gallagher, 2011). Disciplinary, commercial and military listening technologies can, of course, be repurposed for critical, political or artistic ends (e.g. Paglen, 2006), but the reverse is equally true. For example, Pauline Oliveros (2005) presents her deep listening techniques as a means of developing a greater awareness of oneself as part of the sounding world. Yet in the hands of military institutions or 'intelligence' agencies, deep listening might produce very different results.

In summary, I am suggesting that it may be helpful to recognise that listening is both more ambiguous (in relation to meaning) and more ambivalent (in relation to power) than is commonly supposed. This might shift our attention away from simplistic judgments about whether listening is 'genuine' or 'tokenistic', and towards to the affects and the effects of listening; in other words, to questions about what listening *does*.

Selected references

Attali, J. 1985. *Noise: the political economy of music*. Manchester: Manchester University Press.

Benjamin, C. 2002. 'Shot Spotter and FaceIt: The Tools of Mass Monitoring', Los Angeles: University of California *Journal of Law and Technology* 2, pp.1–24, available at http://www.lawtechjournal.com/archives.php.

Blesser, B. And Salter, L-R. 2007. *Spaces speak, are you listening? Experiencing aural architecture*. Cambridge, MA and London: MIT Press.

Daniel, D. 2011. 'Queer sound', *The Wire*, 333, pp.42–46.

Department of Health. 2011. 'Government launches NHS listening exercise', 6 April 2011, available at http://www.dh.gov.uk/en/MediaCentre/DH_125865.

Gallagher, M. 2011. 'Sound, space and power in a primary school' *Social & Cultural Geography* 12, pp.47–61.

Goodman, S. 2009. *Sonic warfare: sound, affect, and the ecology of fear*. Cambridge, MA and London: MIT Press.

Harper, D. 2002. 'Talking about pictures: a case for photo elicitation', *Visual Studies* 17(1), pp.13–26.

LaBelle, B. 2006. *Background noise: perspectives on sound art*. New York and London: Continuum.

Oliveros, P. 2005. *Deep Listening: A Composer's Sound Practice*. New York, Lincoln and Shanghai: iUniverse.

Paglen, T. 2006 'Recording carceral landscapes'. *Leonardo Music Journal* 16, pp.56–57.

Smeaton, A. and McHugh, M. 2006. 'Event detection in an audio-based sensor network', *Multimedia Systems* 12(3), pp.179–194.

Toop, D. 2010. *Sinister resonance: the mediumship of the listener*. New York and London: Continuum.

Veale, A. 2005. 'Creative methodologies in participatory research with children'. In Greene, S. and Hogan, D. (eds.) *Researching children's experience*. Thousand Oaks, CA: Sage, pp.253–272.

Zbikowski, D. 2002. 'The Listening Ear: Phenomena of acoustic surveillance', in Levin, T.Y., Frohne, U. and Weibel, P. (eds.) *CTRL [SPACE] Rhetorics of surveillance from Bentham to Big Brother*. Cambridge, MA and London: MIT Press, pp.33–49.

Rupert Cox

Kill the Inner Voice: Zen and the Self-Conscious Anthropologist

"I await the time of no speech and hear immediately."
Tungshan (807–869) as referred to by the Dôgen (1200–1253)

The anthropologist lies on the gravel path, places an ear to the ground and listens. It is a rainy night in Kyoto city, Japan, and we are in the Zen garden of Taizoin temple. The garden is among the most famous early examples of the dry landscape garden (*karesansui*) in Japan, designed by one of the most important *ishitateso* or 'rock-placing monks', Soseki Muso (1275–1352). The object of the anthropologist's self-conscious auditory posture is an upside down buried water jar (*suikinkutsu*), situated among rocks beside the path and specifically designed to produce distinctive sounds (*suikin'on*). These are the trickling, gurgling sounds of water droplets gathering at the jar's narrow opening and the bell-like resonances as the water strikes its base. The anthropologist places a microphone at the opening of the jar and listening now with earphones, adjusts the levels of a recorder so as to accentuate these particular sonic qualities. The recording will provide detail and, through playback, give an affective presence to the sounds of the *suikinkutsu* that is otherwise difficult to describe ethnographically. There is a Japanese language for describing such sounds as these, which are part of a rich panoply of visual as well as acoustic representational forms in the Japanese Zen Buddhist tradition, but it is in the form of psycho-linguistic puzzles or *kôan* that are directed inwardly towards the dissolution of self and "make no reliance on words or letters" (*furyû monji*). The *kôan* point towards the redundancy of language and rather than substantiate the actuality of a sound, such as that of the *suikinkutsu*, as the object of a self-conscious and self-affirming act of listening, allude to a mode of audition that apprehends spontaneously, without the reason and consequences of conceptualisation, as in this celebrated example:

"Two hands clap and there is a sound: now what is the sound of one hand clapping?" Hakuin Ekaku, 1686–1768

This *kôan* draws attention to the space between the audible and inaudible through silencing or killing the inner voice by which the distinction between a listening subject and an auditory object may be maintained. It involves what the Zen philosopher Dôgen refers to as 'hearing immediately' (*sokumon*) at a time of 'no-speech' (*fugowa*) and can help us to understand other noted auditory features of the Zen garden, such as the *shishi-odoshi*, which is a segmented, pivoted bamboo tube that periodically rotates so as to pour out the constant trickle of water filling one of its chambers and then falls back into place against a rock with a distinctive 'clunk'. Originally designed for somewhat prosaic purposes, to "scare away boar", the auditory delay of this device has come to be appreciated as a contemplative moment for visitors to a Zen garden, referred to by the concept of *ma*, meaning an indeterminate but instantaneously appreciable interval in time or space, that is a 'space between' or 'empty space'.

This concept has been used ambitiously, to explain various artistic endeavours like the editing of the films of the Japanese directors Ozu, Yasuhiro and Iimura Takahiko and the composition of John Cage's Ryôanji music. Used in this way, as an essentialist cultural category, *ma* tends towards the mystification and mythologisation of the specific audio-visual affects of these environments and, like *kôan*, has been subjected in recent years to a radical deconstructive critique of "the rhetoric of immediacy" by the scholar Bernard Faure. This critique finds that rather than being a distraction from experiential immediacy, mediations such as language, ritual and the symbolisation of aural devices such as the *suikinkutsu* and *shishi-odoshi* are integral to the understanding and practice of Zen Buddhism. In this way, the inner voice of the listener in the Zen garden which may compel them to listen but asks "what is it I am listening to?" is like the frustrating, self-conscious attempts of the anthropologist to put a frame around auditory experience through the technological apparatus of a sound recorder; for both reveal a dialectical tension between mediacy and immediacy that is at the core of Zen discourse.

In this sense, the anthropologist's recorder is like the *suikinkutsu* and *shishi-odoshi* and part of a desire to hear and to sonify what cannot be heard, not because it is inaudible, but because it offers the promise of an experience of aural immediacy that lies beyond expression. These devices are therefore necessary distractions, because they draw attention to listening as a sensory modality comprised mutually by the inner voices of mind and matter, and allude to the cacophonous silence of a world of 'absolute nothingness' (*zettai mu*) which lies beyond their sonic objectifications.

For the anthropologist lying on the path of the Zen garden, these considerations mean that their attempt at sound recording has the potential to offer an insight into the act of listening itself, not merely as a reflection on process or positioning, but as a way of listening to their own listening. While such an auditory realisation may not offer a path to enlightenment, for this anthropologist it offered a way to reconcile their self-consciousness with the purpo-se of their investigation.

Francesco López

Wine and dust (excerpt), 2001

[...]

Wine is such a wondrous discovery… I am flying over Mongolia and I can see frozen rivers while I drink Chilean wine and listen to 'Blue Rondo à la Turk'. What is the final outcome of all this? Wine has the answer: it is an enhancer of the soul; it makes me realize instantly that what is driving my perception is actually the broadband sound matter of the plane itself. It contains all the sounds and none of them at the same time. It is a moving micro-environment of normality in an immense sea of raging invisible weather wilderness.

The trip is thus a flowing transfiguration of time and matter, and not just a way of moving from one place to another. A very similar kind of transfiguration to that of the close-up profound listening of all the rivers, seas, mountains, forests, buildings, trains, machines… that preceded this very moment for me. That is, a solipsistic morphing of the potential of 'reality', that—irrelevant?—chimerical environment. And so the plane, the wind, the large masses of crack-ling ice, the slow water below, become the same thing: immaterial ephemeral power that can only be exerted by oneself over oneself; the kind of power that moves me the most and also the most fright-ening of all.

[...]

New York City, after an intense sonic immersion inside mechanical and boiler rooms in office buildings, two killer cocktails: vodka with plum wine, caipirinha with sake. That fine touch of a thin slice of cucumber floating in the clean atmosphere of the glass. Like the high-pitch crispy sounds that swing around the space, freed from the speakers, as I carefully move the EQ faders to create them during the performance. To give them birth from that 'primordial soup' that is the broadband sonic universe. They are born and dead in seconds; they have an ephemeral virtual immaterial life; they are flow, not repetition. And for those who have the innate capability of listening with the spirit, these sounds —as all sounds, for that matter—easily overcome any possible status as signifiers or carriers, becoming beings. Immaterial beings, ungraspable; ghosts of themselves.

Creatures that merge in our perception and travel deep inside us with a precious load of confusing beauty, passion, peacefulness, horror, and other vital elements. Open enhancers of our souls and not just mere servants of language and purpose.

[…]

Near Havana, diving in an underwater cave, I no longer remember the oxygen tank I'm effortlessly carrying with me. No loads or objects to take care of. Instead of that, the overwhelming presence of my breathing; myself as my own environment. Free in the dense slow flight. After the dive, a huge 'Montecristo A' cigar. Powerful, refined, with a presence formed by many layers of taste and smoke. Not simply a very pleasant thing, but, much more importantly, another wondrous discovery in the ancient human quest for richness, detail, delicacy, carefulness and relevance. And all of it slowly vanishing before my eyes; I feel amazed by this.

Like the unexpected sudden clash of melting memories from the sonic density and richness of Tokyo and Patagonia, of crowds and wind. Quickly vanishing and morphing in the weak hands of my memory. But firmly reshaping and invigorating my soul with 'belle confusion'.

For a number of reasons—most of them unknown to me—I dislike possessing material things; their physical presence troubles me in different ways, sometimes in an obsessive manner. The more I like an object, the more I want it to be possessed by someone else. Someone with the courage and skills I lack for keeping material things alive and healthy.

That is, I think, where an important part of my fascination for the work with sound comes from. I have an endless amazement and a profound sense of satisfaction for that intrinsic immateriality of sound 'matter'.

The final materialization of sound dramatically depends upon the sound system used and the actual space where the sounds are projected into. This seems obvious but its consequences at a phenomenological level are rarely acknowledged. Melody, rhythm and words are corrosive agents of phenomenological substance in music. We can recognize the same melody played over a small radio receiver, a huge sound system or simply whistled. But the question is to what extent we give importance to the fact that we are listening to different things.

To me, the beauty and strength of the substance of these 'things' lies upon their vivid physical presence, their potential for mutation and transformation, and their ungraspable ephemeral immateriality. Both a subtle whispering rumour and an overwhelming wall of sound can be created starting from the same encoded sonic information. And both are wonderfully weightless.

'Blank' phenomenological substance is an amazing catalyst for irrational transcendence; to forcefully move away from meaning and purpose. Sonic substance has this potential, and its immateriality is an added virtue for our voyage through the strange path of profound listening. If we want to do such a journey.

[...]

In Dakar the trash is just dust. Like a kind of thin dry dirt. Anything more consistent than that is used in some way or another. Computers are five times as expensive than in the 'first' world, and they have to be covered to be protected from the red dust that quickly impregnates everything.

While I keep recording through the maze of unnamed streets of the large poor suburb of Pikine Icotaf, I admire the ability of the people here to simultaneously keep everything running with almost nothing and to maintain an intuitive joyful spirit towards the cacophony that is being created by all of them. Exactly as I experienced it during other hidden-recording wandering walks in similar places, like the 'medina' of Fes or the 'favela' suburbs in Brasilia.

A couple of weeks later I was in Basse Cassamance, observing the dead body of a monkey completely filled with worms. The whole savannah grassland around me was on fire and I was surrounded by an astonishing mass of crackling sounds from the burning grass. And once again I felt the complex beauty and strength of non-bucolic nature.

[...]

I am laying down on the wet floor of the rain forest in Sarapiquí, Costa Rica. Alone, in complete darkness. Following the activities of the leaf-cutter ants and recording the endless flow of the sonic environment. And I feel like a creator; not because I am recording or because I might be later 'composing' something with these sounds, but simply because I am listening to them with dedication and passion.

Contributors

Moushumi Bhowmik and Sukanta Majumdar have been working together on The Travelling Archive since 2004. The project deals with the field recording, documentation and dissemination of the folk music of Bengal in the east of the Indian subcontinent. Bhowmik is a singer, writer and researcher of Bengali songs who has worked with musicians, authors, filmmakers and theatre directors in India, Bangladesh and the UK. Majumdar is an audiographer who works in cinema and theatre on regional and international productions and also creates works in sound art. They are based in Kolkata. www.thetravellingarchive.org

Sarha Moore is a musician, teacher and PhD student of World Music. She plays saxophone with the Bollywood Brass Band and has played and recorded with highlife, klezmer, jazz, street and big bands. Her PhD research at Sheffield University, 'The Other Leading Note', is a comparative study of the appearance of the phrygian or flat second in raga, maqam, klezmer, heavy metal and western classical music. It assesses the importance of the flat second in music, both structurally and emotionally, and considers how varied associations attributed to it can lead to miscommunication and its use as an Orientalist tool.

Peter Cusack works as a field recordist and sound artist with a special interest in acoustic ecology. He initiated the 'Favourite Sounds Project' that aims to discover what people find positive about their everyday sound environment. His project 'Sounds From Dangerous Places' examines the soundscapes of sites of major environmental damage like Chernobyl and the Caspian oilfields. He produced 'Vermilion Sounds', the environmental sound program for ResonanceFM, and lectures in Sound Arts & Design at the London College of Communication. CDs include Your Favourite London Sounds (Resonance); Baikal Ice (ReR PC2); Favourite Beijing Sounds (KwanYin 022); Sounds from Dangerous Places (ReR PC3&4). favouritesounds.org

Ultra-red is a sound art and popular education collective. Founded in 1994 by two AIDS activists in Los Angeles, Ultra-red's multiple teams conduct sound-based investigations alongside social justice movements in Berlin, London, Torbay, New York and Los Angeles. While the visual image informs much of our understanding of political art, Ultra-red turn the focus to the ear; the sound of communities organising themselves, the acoustics of spaces of dissent, the demands and desires in our voices and silences, the pedagogies of dialogue, the echoes of historical memories of struggle, and a literacy of political listening. www.ultrared.org

Mark Peter Wright is an artist whose work seeks to illuminate understandings of listening and place through detailed use of sound, image and text. His preoccupations with nature, industry, architecture and histories of migration and abandonment have inspired an acclaimed body of work that brings to debate political and cultural aesthetics of subjectivity and place. Wright has exhibited, broadcast and published works across a variety of international venues, festivals, labels and media. In 2009 he received the British Composer of the Year Award [Sonic Arts]. He is also the founder of Ear Room, an online resource co-published by Sound & Music. www.markpeterwright.co.uk

David Toop is a composer/musician, author and curator who has worked in many fields of sound art and music, including improvisation, sound installations, field recordings, pop music production, music for television, theatre and dance. He has published five books, including Ocean of Sound, Haunted Weather, and Sinister Resonance: The Mediumship of the Listener, released eight solo albums, including Screen Ceremonies, Black Chamber and Sound Body, and as a critic has written for many publications, including The Wire, The Face, Leonardo Music Journal and Bookforum Exhibitions he has curated include Sonic

Boom at the Hayward Gallery, London, *Playing John Cage* at Arnolfini, Bristol, and *Blow Up* at Flat-Time House, London. Visiting Professor at Leeds College of Music, he is a Senior Research Fellow at London College of Communication.

Dr. Michael Gallagher is a research associate in human geography at the University of Glasgow. His current research involves experimentation with audio and other media as methods for engaging with environments, people and places. Previous to this, he has written extensively on research with children and young people. He also makes experimental music as part of the duo 'Buffalo buffalo buffalo Buffalo buffalo' and produces minimal techno records anonymously.
www.michaelgallagher.co.uk

Rupert Cox has been a lecturer in social anthropology at the University of Manchester, UK since 2003. He works on the anthropology of sound, investigating questions about the politics of noise from the perspectives of acoustic science, sound studies and sound art, and focuses on projects in Japan. His original research into sound matters arose from questions about the nature of Zen experience and the famous koan 'What is the sound of one hand clapping?'. Having worked on the 'Air Pressure' project that led to an exhibition and CD, he is now using sound recordings and film to investigate the idea of military aircraft sound as a 'Sound of Freedom' focusing on the US military bases in Okinawa. The Sound of Freedom research will be the basis of a Berg monograph due for publication in 2014.

Francisco López is internationally recognised as one of the main figures on the stage of sound art and experimental music. His experience in the field of sound creation and work with environmental recordings covers a period of more than 30 years, during which he has developed an impressive sound universe that is completely personal and iconoclastic and based on profound listening to the world. He has realised hundreds of sound installations, projects with field recordings, and concerts/performances in 60 countries, including at the main international concert halls, museums, galleries and festivals. His extensive catalogue of sound pieces (with live and studio collaborations with more than 150 international artists) has been published by more than 250 recording companies all over the world. He has been awarded honorary mentions at the Ars Electronica Festival (Austria) four times and is the recipient of the Qwartz Award 2010 (France) for best sound compilation.
www.franciscolopez.net

Listening Spaces

Most of the essays in this section discuss 'eventscapes' where either one species or one specialised area of activity dominates, often making it difficult for us to access the acoustic space. Even if we are able to listen, in many acoustic environments—even those made and inhabited primarily by humans—our ability and desire to interpret, decode, analyse and describe what we hear is neither highly developed nor, in general, valued.

Many of the contributors in the following section write of experiences of listening to specific acoustic spaces from both above and below. They share concerns ranging from issues of ownership and control with related ecological, social and political repercussions to the insights that listening can offer into worlds which are hidden from sight.

David Rothenberg reminds us that the now famous song of the humpbacked whale was discovered relatively recently, revealed by new technology that opened up the underwater world to human hearing. We do not, however, know for certain whether whales listen to themselves—something that Rothenberg is probing in his musical improvisations with these mammals. Gianni Pavan's explanation of aspects of his research highlights concerns about the effects, particularly changes in sound-making habits, on species who inhabit underwater environments made increasingly noisy by human activity. Above water, people who make a living from the sea have developed techniques of listening to help them build up a picture of the seabed beneath them. Penny Howard describes the multi-sensory nature of fishing where the whole body is used to sense changing vibrations that might suggest the presence, size and kind of fish in the unseen depths.

Even above the ground, listening is often the best way of sensing and knowing. Andrew Whitehouse meditates on why hearing is not considered good enough and seeing is still believing. He illustrates this with tales of the crake family, a variety of bird with distinctive calls which can rarely be seen owing to their behaviour and preferred habitat. He suggests that in the past hearing was more valued as a sensory mode and wonders how different the world might be if this were still the case. This theme is expanded by Blesser and Salter who point out the difference between the 'eventscape' and the 'objectscape', concluding that "what you see is not necessarily where you are". Like Howard, they refer to human visualisation of objects through listening to the environment and how humans use technology to create their own 'eventscape'. Ross Brown describes this from a personal point of view in his daily cycle commute through London, when he enhances and controls his listening environment through listening to music on headphones while still being able to hear the information he needs for safe cycling. He extends this creation of a space for listening from the personal to the design and building of theatrical auditoria, places constructed for a specific kind of listening experience. Daniela Cascella also writes from a personal perspective using her situated listening experiences at the Protestant Cemetery in Rome to meditate on how listening is so much more than hearing the environment, informed as it is by other listenings, readings and writings as she searches for the words to capture and encompass the specific character of the space she comes both to listen in and to arrive at through her listening. In a similar vein, Jérôme Joy discusses how the merging of listening experiences and states that we encounter in music might be able to help us to construct ideal listening environments.

The remaining three contributors address in different ways the knowledge that listening can give rise to. Meri Kytö's diary of her situated listenings does not describe them or what she heard but tells us what they told her and what she learnt from these experiences. Jean-Paul Thibaud is concerned with what we could learn from listening to others in public space; in this case the ambient soundscape of Largo da Carioca in Rio de Janeiro. He argues for an 'ethnophony' of ambience or more particularly of the situated voice or voices in a specific space. From many people, many voices and many events to one—Steve Rowell's description of his project in the Mohave desert, an environment primarily inhabited by non-human species, where a number of times a day human intervention totally dominates the acoustic environment with an acoustic event far in excess of its visual equivalent, that reminds us of how often it is humans whose control and domination can hugely impact on the sonic environment in ways we often cannot merely know through seeing.

David Rothenberg

Playing Along With Whales

Aia no i ka mea e mele ana, as the ancient Hawaiians said—"Let the singer select the song". And so they do, changing their songs from year to year, with each male humpback singing exactly the same song. If they all want to sound the same, why do they change it? We don't know. Almost everything about humpback whale song we do not know. It is the longest, most beautiful musical performance of any animal, and humans never mentioned hearing it until the end of the 1950s, when the US Navy dropped giant underwater microphones, hydrophones, deep down under the surface and picked up strange organised sound that they hoped were secret enemy transmissions. Unfortunately for them, the sounds turned out to be coming from humpback whales. Immediately they knew what

to do—tell no one. "We can't let people find out about this", muttered the admiral. And they didn't release recordings of these beautiful songs until ten years later, in the heart of the sixties, when the hippies were ready for them. Once the song was out it spread all across the

globe to become the best-selling nature recording of all time. It led to the Save the Whales movement which has turned most of the world's peoples against whaling, save rogue nations like Norway, Iceland, and Japan. Before the popularity of whale music, nobody cared.

At least that's how the story goes. "Would that these great silent beasts be able to talk?" wondered Melville more than a hundred years back. "What marvellous tales they would tell." And yet, if you dive not so deep under the waters in a place full of singing humpbacks during mating season, say the waters off Maui in early spring, it is easy for the unaided ear to hear humpback song. Faint and muffled for sure, but unequivocally there. If any diver can hear it, why did no one notice the mournful, deep, emotional songs of humpback whales until technology told us it was there? This is one of those great mysteries of human perception, and I have no certain answer. But it is as if no one thought to listen for such songs under water since we did not expect them to be there. Expecting silence, we find silence. And yet the ocean is a sonically pulsing, thrumming world.

To play clarinet along with humpback whales is a strange and marvellous thing. I sit aboard a sailboat or a motor boat with the engine turned off, toss down my hydrophone, put on the headphones.

I'll always hear noisy, fluid sounds, either the snapping of shrimp or the thlack of waves against the boat and the rocks. If there are whales, they will usually be a vast chorus of animals near and far. Sound travels so well underwater that whales ten miles away will still sound pretty close. The best situation is to be right near one loud singing male. Then there is a chance that a musical encounter will happen.

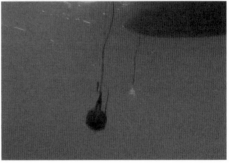

Next I drop down a small submersible speaker, attached to a 40 watt battery-powered amp. I place a microphone in front of the clarinet on the boat, and then I begin to play, listening to the headphones to what happens in the sonic world down below. The whale is singing there, and my clarinet joins in, sounding muffled, with extra overtones, more bell-like, a bit distorted, something like a saxophone blaring through the deep water void.

Often the whale will ignore me, and just keep singing what he was singing before. Kind of like a lot of improvising musicians I know! But sometimes he will appear to change his song, respond to what I play, strive to match it at times, or alternate with a call-and-response to fill in the blanks. I don't have enough evidence to know for sure whether humpback whales can change their song in response to what a clarinet plays, but in the best examples, I really do feel I hear it. On my piece 'Never Satisfied' on the *Whale Music* CD you can hear for yourself what goes on in one special live clarinet/humpback duet. That's the best one I ever recorded. It's named after scientist Jim Darling's research boat, since he's never satisfied with the results he's gotten so far. The true scientist can never rest on his laurels, but must always go out again and again to collect more data. Darling has tried to watch what happens when humpback whales sing for more than a decade. Since only the male whales sing, most scientists assume this musical behaviour has evolved to attract the attention of female whales. Except how many times have people ever seen female humpbacks respond visibly to the song? Never. Not even once, in a few decades of observation.

What Darling did find is that in 86% of the instances where anything visible happened at all, a second male whale will approach a singing whale, then the first will stop singing. The two will swim next to each other in silence for several minutes, then separate once more. When they are a least a kilometre apart, they will each start singing again.

Will the song be changed? Is this how new music is passed between the great cetaceans—in silence!? Once again, we don't know.

Whale song science is hard, devilishly difficult. You have to wait years to record enough examples of meaningful encounters for the data to matter at all. Music works differently; all I need is one great connection between a whale musician and a human musician to suggest that music can cross species lines, that a song can be sung and played that is part-human, another part whale. The pelagic beauty of such a possibility crosses whole oceans with its rarity and surprise. I have caught it once in a while, but more often than not no musical connection happens at all.

Such is the travail of making music underwater, from the land world of people to the water world of whales. It is indeed a crazy prospect, likely to make imbalanced music no species will tolerate!

Except music is special, it transports meaning even if the mechanism behind it remains unknown. We do not know why music works, why we value it so much, or how melodies can encode so much emotion that humpback whale songs easily make people of all ages cry.

There is beauty in the sea down deep below us. Through our music we can touch it and sometimes, yes, in those best times, we might just change the way a great whale sings.

Penny McCall Howard

Feeling the Ground: Vibration, Listening, Sounding at Sea

Compared to the sea he or she works in, the body of a fisherman is a tiny, insignificant thing. Moreover, most of the work of catching fish or prawns occurs far below the boat, in an environment fishermen cannot see and have never directly experienced. Effective work at sea requires an extraordinary extension of the whole body's sensitivities and perceptual abilities, and merges feeling, listening, sounding, and seeing.

Skipper 'Buckie' John concentrated intently with his whole body while trawling over rough ground. Putting his hand on the wheelhouse wall he would reach down to the seafloor far below along the bar-taut wires that extended through the boat's wake made roiling and turbulent by heavy gear towed at great depths. 'Buckie' John felt the vibration of his fishing gear from the wheelhouse, along the deck of the boat, up onto the steel structure taking the strain of the trawl net, down 150 metres of trawl wire and finally to the hoppers at the front of the net as they bumped along the sea floor. The wheelhouse window gave a particularly precise feel for the vibration that was omnipresent on a small engine-powered boat and which could also be felt through

Looking from the boat into the sea along the wires attached to the trawl net.

the soles of the feet or through the wheelhouse chair. At the same time as 'Buckie' John felt the ground, he watched it on the electronic depth sounder over his right shoulder. Just out of the picture his right hand rested on the engine controls ready to "give it the handle" and accelerate the engine should he feel the fishing gear "sticking". Using such extended techniques for feeling, the skipper was able to access information far beyond the immediate reach of his senses and carry out work in an environment in which human survival would be impossible for more than a few minutes.

In the air, hearing is usually accomplished through sensing vibration within the ear and listening to it (Ingold describes some important exceptions, see 2000: 271-274). But in the water, sound is vibration felt with the whole body (Helmreich, 2007: 264). Sounds or vibrations are also transmitted through other solids immersed in the sea—like the hull of a ship—to be heard and felt by those living and travelling on boats floating at the surface. The crew of old whaling ships describe hearing sounds of the ocean and its creatures eerily echo through the hull of the ship. These motions and vibrations are also heard in the rumble of the engine and the crashing and clattering of objects tossed about.

Listening as feeling

A trawler at sea is also an incredibly noisy place and every sound is significant. Yet these sounds were interpreted not so much by listening as by extended techniques for feeling with the whole body, combined with a constant adjustment of tools, machines, and enormous weights and tensions. New crew needed an 'education of attention' (Gibson, 1979: 254) in order to 'feel the ground' and react appropriately in order to "keep the trawl going". They had to learn to distinguish the

'Feeling the ground' through the boat and fishing gear.

vibrations coming through the fishing gear from the ground from the constant noise and vibration of the engine, the whine of the electronics, and the shuddering and slamming of the boat itself on the waves. Fishermen used these techniques to work productively and also to develop complex descriptions and visualisations of what their fishing gear and the seafloor far below looked like. Although fishermen watched everything and everyone above the surface intently, below the surface direct vision was regarded as the least useful of the senses. One successful young skipper gave me his copy of the video that scientists made of prawns on the seafloor, explaining that it was no use to him. Another skipper who had previously worked diving for scallops told me there was nothing that he saw in his diving that was of much use in fishing for prawns.

Feeling and listening have a long history of being used at sea to orient oneself and to locate other objects or organisms. One man described to me how in thick fog going through the narrows of Loch Hourn, his father would shout out of the wheelhouse window and use the echo of his voice bouncing off the cliffs to tell where he was. This kind of human echolocation is not unique to the sea; for example, John Hull has described the use of echolocation by those who are blind, gaining a form of sight out of sound (Hull, 2005: 324, discussed in Ingold, 2000: 271–272).

In the herring fishery, Martin describes the historic practice of listening for the *plub*[1] of a single herring on dark silent nights, men with hands cupped to ears, young boys "castigated repeatedly until silence became, for them too, habitual", and the preference for boats built with the type of planking considered to be quieter when wavelets lapped against it (Martin, 1981: 164).[2] On days when they were fishing close to shore and "the weather was too loud for herring to be heard", a pole would be held in the water to feel for herring striking it and to assess the density of the shoal (Martin, 1981: 172). When phosphorescent phytoplankton became more abundant in the summer and autumn, a sharp bang of a metal anchor on the wooden gunwhale of the boat would send vibrations through the water and the herring would start, producing a flash in the phosphorescence that was termed "answering the anchor" (Martin, 1981: 164). The flash, or deep-down glow, of an 'answering shoal' was used to distinguish the size of individual fish, the species, and the size of the overall shoal (Martin, 1981: 164–6). When John McWhirter describes the incessant knocking of anchors sounding the deep, it is hard not to think of the depth sounders incessantly pinging away in today's sea:

> Ye wid sweir there wis two or three shipbuilding yerds working, anchors goin' the whole night, chappin', chappin', the whole night. It wis a wonder there wis a herring lef above at aaa'. Quietness tae [till] the burnin' [phosphorescent plankton] came in the waater, an'

1. The Gaelic term for a single complete herring jump, used by the fishermen on the Mull of Kintyre on the south-west coast of Scotland.
2. The overlapping planking of clinker-built boats were considered noiser due to the lapping of waves against the ridged hull, and therefore more likely to confuse the sounds of herring than those of smooth carvel-planked boats (Martin 1981: 164).

as soon as the burning came in the waater, a man furrid [forward on the boat] wi' his anchor. (Martin, 1981: 166)

The ambiguity between modes of sensory perception was expressed by Hugh MacFarlane, who explained that "They *felt* wan jump [a herring], they winna hear it". These fishermen would use the expression to "feel herring", when, as Martin describes it, "the obvious meaning was 'hear', 'smell', or 'see'" (1981: 172).

In the 1930s boats began to target herring lying in deeper water. Swedish fishermen working in Scottish waters used a 'feeling-wire' to find herring in this deeper water, and its use spread to the Scottish fishermen. The wire was made of twine, later piano wire, with a weight on the end, and would be held on the thumb or fore-finger (Martin, 1981: 228). With experience the wire could be used to estimate the depth and density of a shoal of herring, and to distinguish different species of fish. When the man wiring "felt them thick" he would call the skipper (Martin, 1981: 229). Johnny *'Beag'* explained:

They would have a line off the bow of the boat and the boat would be moving slowly along and they could feel the shoal of fish... the line must have vibrated when you came up against the shoal of herring... The same with the mackerel, but mackerel are a lot at the surface, they play on the surface, and they move very, very fast, but herring, they were just shoals of herring and they could feel just the tremor on the line so they knew they were into a shoal.

Listening, feeling, and seeing overlapped and were used in particular circumstances to enable people to become fully engaged with, imagine, and work in places they could not see or directly experience. 'Feeling' the herring was accomplished with their ears or hands or a finger, using a pole or a wire or thousands of phosphorescent organisms, and sometimes 'seeing' the land meant listening for a shout echoing off a cliff. Sensing was transductive, across media (Helmreich, 2007)—the pole and the wire reaching beyond and far below the surface of the water, the bang of an anchor transformed into a flash of herring, and the crew spring-ing into action.

Techniques for sounding like those used by the herring fishermen and 'Buckie' John now incorporate electronic depth sounders. Users experience sounders as 'seeing' and even 'feeling' the seafloor, challenging the boundaries between senses. The transducers of electronic depth sounders send pulses and clicks through the water, which travel to bounce off solid objects and return. Sound measures time which a small computer converts into distance and displays as light in a moving pixelated image on a screen.[3] Images are interpreted in conjunction with feeling the vibrations of tensioned fishing gear, and combined with immediate bodily reaction and labour in a vivid three-dimensional imagination that is constantly put to work and tested.

A fisherman described using his first depth sounder in the 1970s as a kind of revelation, because "You could tell, *off* the shore, where there was hard rock on the bottom". The most important quality of the sounder was to be able to 'see' the character of the seafloor before your gear got there, and fishermen like 'Buckie' John used the sounder in conjunction with feeling his gear. The experience of using a depth sounder could cross over into direct feeling, which I experienced in a visceral way one evening. Dusk was falling, and a fisherman generously led me out of the complicated entrance of a small harbour in his small motor boat. He glided to a stop and asked me what my sounder said. It was now very dark, the rocks and land disappearing and merging into the blackening sky. If I turned on a light on the boat I would be blinded. I told him the depth and he told me that "What you will see on your sounder is the bottom will drop away to about 80 metres, and then it will come back up really sharply. Don't worry! It will just level out at about 20 metres." He turned away and I carried on through the darkness. I watched the bottom fall away, and then its heart-stopping rise. The thing I most wanted to know is where the bottom was and I stared at the depth sounder intently. But the reason I wanted to know where the bottom lay was because I wanted to keep it away. I started to imagine with dread what I would do if I ran the boat aground just now, on a falling tide with a gale coming up tomorrow. More than anything, I felt like a person feeling along a wall in the dark, reaching out to touch something in order to keep it away, to hold it at a safe distance. But it was the sounder I was feeling the seafloor with. Despite the ethereal and digitally processed nature of the sound waves that connected me to the seafloor, for that hour at least, it was as if I was reaching out to touch it.[4]

For 'Buckie' John and for me there was no radical distinction between what was felt through the boat or heard with the ears

3. In the 1970s the display would have been a light that flashed on at the number that corresponded to a particular depth, with 2 or more flashes indicating a denser bottom. Today most sounders have colour displays on an LCD screen where colour indicates the density of the seafloor. Red is the most dense.

4. The question was raised with me whether this experience was a function of my own inexperience. Commenting on a draft of this chapter, trawler skipper Alasdair told me, unprompted, that he thought my description was 'spot on' and similar to experiences he remembered with both a sounder and the radar in the fog.

or seen on the sounder, just like the old herring fishermen who "*felt* wan jump, they winna hear it" (Martin, 1981: 171). It was the attentiveness of one's whole body which allowed one to 'get in' to challenging ground, or feel the bottom at night. The techniques fishermen use to extend their bodies to sound and feel the depths, to work in and develop the affordances of places they cannot see and have never visited must combine multiple forms of perception. This full sensory attentiveness is perhaps parallel to a blind person for whom, "the body itself has become the organ of sense" (Hull, 2005: 326), but in this case, it is a body that is also extended hundreds of meters beneath the sea's surface.

Selected references

Gibson, James J. 1979. *The Ecological Approach to Visual Perception*. London: Houghton Mifflin.

Helmreich, Stefan. 2007. 'An anthropologist underwater: Immersive soundscapes, submarine cyborgs, and transductive ethnography'. *American Ethnologist*. 34: pp.621–641.

Hull, John. 2005. 'Rainfall and the Blind Body', in *The Book of Touch*. Edited by Constance Classen, pp.324–327. Oxford: Berg.

Ingold, Tim. 2000. *The Perception of the Environment: Essays in livelihood, dwelling, skill*. London: Routledge.

Martin, Angus. 1981. *The Ring-Net Fishermen*. Edinburgh: John Donald Publishers.

Gianni Pavan

Listening Underwater

Listening to the submarine world is a fascinating experience.
However, our ears are not well suited for underwater hearing and
thus we must rely on specific instruments—hydrophones—to discover
underwater sounds. Hydrophones receive the acoustic waves in a
wide range of frequencies, from few Hertz (Hz) to many hundred Kilo-
hertz (kHz), much more than the human ear can perceive. The first
investigations into underwater sound were conducted by military
navies in an effort to detect and locate enemy ships and submarines
by listening to the noise of their engines and propellers. The equipment developed for military needs allowed unexpected biological
sounds to be heard; these puzzled the experts for many years and
opened up new scientific research branches: acoustical oceanography
and marine bioacoustics.

In the aquatic environment, acoustic communication among
animals has a very important role because the high propagation
speed (about 1500 m/sec—almost five times greater than in air) and
the scarce attenuation with distance allow an efficient transmission
of the sounds. Many species use sounds not only to communicate but
also to explore the environment around them. Sight, that is limited
to a few metres in water and that can't be used in the dark oceanic
depths, is thus replaced by the use of sound.

Many aquatic organisms produce sounds. Invertebrates (crustaceans, aquatic insects), fishes, frogs, reptiles, marine mammals
(cetaceans and pinnipeds) produce sounds with frequencies ranging
from infrasounds to ultrasounds. Sound production in crustaceans
and fishes is common but remains little studied. In Teleost fishes
more than 50 families include species that use sounds to communicate, normally with frequencies below a few kHz and low sound
intensity that limits the communication range to short distances.
On the contrary, cetaceans use sound extensively, with sound levels
that allow communication over long ranges, and ultrasonic acoustic pulses that allow accurate echo-location over ranges of many
hundred of metres.

Marine bioacoustics is the study of the sounds produced by marine
animals, to understand their behaviour and their relationships with

the marine environment. Beyond studying individual features of each species for their biological and ecological significance, marine bioacoustics is also concerned with the development of practical applications for the management and preservation of the environment.

Marine Mammals

The zoological group of marine mammals includes animals who live underwater as well as terrestrial animals who spend only part of their time in water, for feeding, for example. Sirenians (manatees and dugongs), Pinnipeds (seals, sea-lions and walruses), otters and Cetaceans spend all or most of their life in water and use sound extensively.

Cetaceans are divided into two sub-orders, the Odontocete, or toothed whales, and the Mysticete, or baleen whales, each one with peculiar behaviours and acoustic features. Auditory mechanisms and sound producing organs are highly evolved and diversified with the acquisition of the ability to echo-locate (biosonar or biological sonar), which is peculiar to the Odontocete and among other animals has only reached an equivalent level of sophistication in bats (Chiroptera).

The underwater environment has its own acoustic peculiarities and cetaceans are extraordinarily well adapted to them. In these mammals, acoustic communication has acquired a privileged role compared to other channels of communication. Their extraordinary sensory and cognitive skills have allowed them to successfully exploit the marine environment and to evolve as top predators by using acoustics.

Their signals range spectrally from the very low frequencies of the large baleen whales to the ultrasonic clicks of the echo-locating dolphins. Dolphins produce ultrashort biosonar signals (30 to 300 μsec) that reach peak source levels of 230 dB re 1μPa/1m and range from 70 kHz to more than 150 kHz, while social communication usually happens at lower frequencies but still impressive intensities. Other than echo-location clicks, most Odontocetes produce tonal whistles for communication at frequencies lower than those used for echo-location.

The Mysticetes are filter feeders feeding on plankton and small fish and are primarily the larger whales, ranging in size from 8 up to 28 metres. Because they do not need to chase their prey they have not developed echo-location. Their sounds are mainly low frequency tonals for inter-individual communication although there is evidence that some whales can transmit an FM sweep that can be potentially used to capture a large scale 'acoustic image' of the surrounding environment. As low frequencies propagate well into water, baleen whale sounds may propagate for hundreds of kilometres.

The distance of detection of cetacean sounds varies widely, depending on signal characteristics and environmental constraints, including background noise, most of which is caused by increasing everyday human activities (such as ship traffic, naval sonar, geophysical surveys, oceanographic instruments, offshore platforms and offshore wind farms).

Underwater sound and its analysis

Hydrophones are the transducers that transform sounds propagating underwater into electrical signals that can be recorded and then analyzed. They are usually omni-directional and may cover a wide range of frequencies, from a few Hz to more than 100 kHz. More complex hydrophone systems consisting of multiple transducers are also used, typically to locate acoustic sources. In marine bioacoustics, the hydrophones used are mostly stationary, for the monitoring of a given area, or towed for continuous monitoring during navigation. For some applications, they may be packaged with a recorder and batteries to operate autonomously for periods of time extending from a few hours to months. These devices can be deployed on the sea bottom, or, if small enough, attached to an animal. Cetacean sounds detected by hydrophones may be visualised and analysed in real time, and/or recorded for later processing.

In marine bioacoustics, the most advanced research investigates the neurophysiology and behaviour of marine mammals to understand how these animals have developed their acoustic capabilities, how they interpret the signals they receive from the environment and if, and how, they are impacted by the noise generated by human activity. These research activities are driven by conservation needs and by an increasing concern about the impact of anthropogenic noise at both individual and population levels. Current research aims to develop continuous monitoring of the underwater acoustic environment to measure noise levels and marine biodiversity by recognizing the acoustic features of each marine mammal species.

Selected references

Webb J. F., Popper A. N. and Fay R. R. 2008. *Fish Bioacoustics*. New York: Springer.

Au W. W. L. and Hastings M. C. 2008. *Principles Of Marine Bioacoustics*. New York: Springer.

Richardson W. J., Greene C. R. Jr., Malme C. J. and Thomson D. H., 1995. *Marine Mammals And Noise*. San Diego: Academic Press.

Obrist M. K., Pavan G., Sueur J., Riede K., Llusia D. and Márquez R. 2010. 'Bioacoustic approaches in biodiversity inventories' in *Manual on Field Recording Techniques and Protocols for All Taxa Biodiversity Inventories*. Brussels: Abc Taxa. Vol. 8: pp.68–99. Available online: http://www.abctaxa.be/volumes/volume-8-manual-atbi/volumes/volume-8-manual-atbi/chapter-5

Andrew Whitehouse

Living Doubts: The Ontology of Hearing, Seeing and Naming Birds

In certain parts of Europe a sound that can be heard during the summer months is the dry and repetitive call of a corncrake. This was once a familiar sound to many, but the bird has declined enormously over the past century in the face of agricultural intensification. I've heard corncrakes on numerous occasions, particularly in Islay in western Scotland, a remaining stronghold for the species. But, much to my frustration, I've never seen one. They're skulking birds that live in grassy fields and dry marshland,[1] where they remain almost constantly invisible and, try as I might, they've never even shown their heads above the tops of the grass when I've been looking. As John Clare famously wrote in his poem about the corncrake, 'The Landrail',

> Tis like a fancy everywhere
> A sort of living doubt
> We know tis something but it neer
> Will blab the secret out

Crakes are found elsewhere in the world too, and present similar challenges to anyone who seeks to observe them. During a two-month stay at the Reserva Ecologica de Guapiaçu in Brazil, I heard plenty in the extensive beds of rushes where the chances of seeing them were slender. The strange and sometimes rather un-birdlike calls of different species were pointed out to me by rangers or visiting birders: the excitable trilling of rufous-sided crake, the exhilarating duet of ash-throated crake and the shrill squeal of their near relative the blackish rail. Perhaps my favourite was the almost electrical rush of russet-crowned crake, brilliantly described in one field guide as "like the sound of a seashell wind chime or someone going through a bead curtain" (van Perlo, 2009: 92). Later, I was able to compare what I'd heard with pre-existing recordings and so was able to confirm that I'd heard 'the right sounds'. With patience

I was eventually able to see all of these birds, but I rarely saw them making the sounds attributed to them. For most birds it's sooner or later possible to observe them vocalising, but crakes present an altogether greater challenge, a challenge that raises some important questions about sounds and naming, or more specifically that process of naming called 'identification'.

So how do I identify a sound as being a particular crake? How does one know that a sound is made by a certain kind of bird if one has never seen the bird making that sound? In one sense I know that I'm hearing crakes in the same way that I 'know' the Earth is spherical. Like most people I've never seen the Earth as a sphere (although I've seen plenty of two-dimensional images of this of course), but I go along with the conventional understanding of its roundness even though this isn't something I've experienced directly. Perhaps if I had training in astrophysics I would be able to perceive the effects of the Earth's spherical shape all the time but, as it is, I've never seen the Earth as a whole and nor have I seen a corncrake making that rasping sound.

Identification might provisionally be understood as a process of naming that links direct perception with a conventionalised classificatory system. In knowing that the sound I'm hearing is being made by a species of bird named corncrake, I'm fitting a particular sense experience into a pre-existing matrix of taxonomic differences that is based on knowledge accumulated through the work of many others. My skill at naming the sound as 'a corncrake' is still reliant on a wider external knowledge of how that sound connects with certain birds and how those birds are differentiated from others. One can thus conceive of identification as involving attempts to relate the subjective with the objective and the particular with the general. Following this understanding of identification, learning to identify birds and their sounds is as much about learning the system as it is about learning how to 'listen carefully'.

But why all the fuss about seeing? 'Seeing is believing' is the saying, but why is this? One of the cornerstones of our ontology is the idea that the world is filled with objects and that sounds have their source in the actions of these objects. Applying this to the case in question, 'crex crex' is a sound made by an object we call a corncrake. The sound is not the bird, rather it is made by the bird. And conventionally the bird is only apprehended *as an object* through our *seeing it*. These ontological assumptions help to explain why birders, like me, are so keen to see birds. It's only through seeing, we assume, that we perceive 'the bird'. Hearing a bird, in this way of thinking, is no different to seeing its nest or its tracks. They are made by the bird, but they are not the bird itself.

But is this the only way to think about sounds, or indeed our experience of the world more generally? What if we were to think of the sound as being the bird, just as much as the assemblage of feathers and bone that we conventionally think makes the sound? Such a way of thinking is not so uncommon amongst other peoples, and I suspect it was once more conventional amongst our ancestors, as is reflected in the prominence of onomatopoeic vernacular names. The way we name birds can reflect on how we think about and perceive them. It's much easier to think of a sound as the bird if it has an onomatopoeic name. In fact the name 'crake' is onomatopoeic of the corncrake (which even has an onomatopoeic scientific name: *Crex crex*), although when applied to the South American crakes it's less helpful. To give a more familiar example, when one 'hears the cuckoo', one is directly perceiving the bird. 'Seeing the cuckoo' makes a bit less sense, until it becomes conventionalised as the name of a family of birds (see Ingold, 2000). I saw several kinds of cuckoo in Brazil, but never heard a single 'cuckoo'.

Onomatopoeic names have never found great favour with the taxonomists who work to standardise English bird names, perhaps because names that resemble the sounds of birds are not easy to render hierarchically. For example, the English names of South American birds are almost always structured in the same binomial fashion as scientific names and rarely refer to their sounds. This is despite the majority of species being forest dwellers that are more easily noticed and recognised by their vocalising than through visual encounters. The preference for hierarchical names requires us to primarily understand birds according to their relation to the classificatory system composed of families; one's perceptions in the field become relegated to this structure. But a preference for onomatopoeic names might help to draw the sound and the bird together in such a way that de-emphasises the hierarchical narrative of biological taxonomy. Indeed, I would suggest we might go further even than 'cuckoo' or 'crake'. In those cases the sounds are still nouns that lead us to think of an object, either in sound or substance. What if the names were verbs that reflect activity rather than objectivity (Ingold, 2005: 163)? Of course some bird names reflect their activities —woodpecker, warbler, and so on—but these are rendered as agent nouns, as if the bird is fulfilling a job description. What if we had 'cuckooing' or 'craking'? In this sense the name would be what the bird does; the bird would not be an object that makes sounds but a centre of activity in its environment. The bird would then become what it does, rather than that activity following from what it already is or the role it fulfils. Identifying birds would thus become an ongoing process of perception, rather than fitting perceived features into a pre-existing order.

Selected references

Ingold, T. 2000. *The perception of the environment: essays on livelihood, dwelling and skill.* London: Routledge.

Ingold, T. 2005. 'Naming as storytelling: speaking of animals among the Koyukon of Alaska', in A. Minelli, G. Ortalli and G. Sanga (eds.), *Animal names*. Venice: Istituto Veneto di Scienze, Lettere ed Arti, 2005, pp.159–172.

Lorimer, J. 2008. 'Counting corncrakes: the affective science of the UK corncrake census', *Social Studies of Science* 38 (3): pp.377–405.

Van Perlo, B. 2009. *A field guide to the birds of Brazil*. Oxford: Oxford University Press.

Jean-Paul Thibaud

Giving Voice to Urban Atmospheres

Largo da Carioca in downtown Rio de Janeiro on a hot November afternoon. A disconcerting experiment with one very simple instruction: cross this square blindfolded with the help of an attentive guide and, at the same time, describe one's immediate sensations and impressions. This means walking as if blind for about 20 minutes and having your impressions recorded. The experiment produces a series of sound recordings featuring the voice of the blind stroller along with the noises from Largo da Carioca in the background. Note the stifling heat and the uneven ground… impressions that isolate the cries of hawkers and the noise of traffic… all sorts of remarks that attempt to put into words what is perceived and felt along the way.

However, what if we also listened to the voices themselves, their melody and rhythm, their hesitations, intonations, laughing, silence, exclamations and interjections, the intermittent vocal flows that describe the body in motion to the keen ear? What if we focused on the textures and sounds of the spoken word with its different inflections, dynamics and accents? What if we paid greater attention to the perceptible hum of background vocals on the recording? This could be presented in terms of the voice as expression and production of ambiences or—better still—the *ambient voice*.

In addition to what is actually said—that is, the semantic content —we are attempting to listen to the musicality of the spoken word from the perspective of the senses. We are not interested in the timbre of the voice itself as the signature of a specific body, but in the variations and fluctuations of the voice in a situation, as shifts taking place in an ambience. So this involves giving vent to to the sensitive body in one's dealings with the ambient environment; the effort and undertaking of movement; the affective tonalities of experiences in progress and problems encountered; adjusting the voice to what is heard; paying attention to certain events; maintaining contact with the interlocutor, and so on. In a nutshell, a myriad of phonic 'gestures' that accompany and embody public life and render the dynamics of places, flows, publics and exchanges audible. Without attempting to compile an exhaustive list, here are four types of particularly clear and striking phonic 'gestures'.

Capturing gesture: a first listening reveals gestures that aim to *capture the attention* of passers-by. During the walk across the square, a series of interjections punctuates the descriptions that make it possible to start another comment. Speech does not flow in an unbroken manner but leaves room for silences of varying lengths depending on the nature and diversity of the surrounding stimuli. These speech-triggers—"ha!", "well…", "here…" highlight those moments and the mechanisms through which the attention of passers-by is secured. All that is needed is street music or the hailing of a street seller somewhere in the soundscape for the passer-by to suddenly enter a darker zone where they encounter an obstacle to being able to speak again. There are also cases where speech is merely suspended: the passer-by has momentarily stopped speaking but continues to study an event or a phenomenon without putting it into words. Silence here indicates that the focus of attention is in progress, a lingering focus on what has been noticed that makes it more difficult to speak at the same time; for example, when one hears other passers-by gradually approaching and then moving away. Because the ambience in Largo da Carioca is a stimulating and dynamic one, it throws up frequent and diverse capturing gestures and gives rise to numerous micro events and shifts in attention. We can define it here as an amplified attention-grabbing space.

Articulation gesture: a second listening points up articulation gestures that reveal practical ways of *physical engagement*. This time the voice gives expression to a body in motion with all its tensions, fluidity and inertia—movements and series of movements. As an acoustic body, it extends and accompanies, renders and reinitialises the physical engagement involved in crossing the square. As such, although Largo itself does not leave much of a vocal trace along the way—the fluidity of the recording prevails here—this is not true at the periphery. The broken footpaths and uneven surfaces give rise to a rhythmical and melodious modulation of speech. Merely stepping up onto the path becomes audible and bears out the effort made by the passer-by. The voice takes part in the strollers' physical engagement and merely expresses what is being accomplished in its own way and this allows us to retrace the entire crossing of Largo step by step, word by word. The crossing is quite bumpy at its outer limits but easier on the actual square itself and not especially challenging physically.

For present purposes, Largo may be defined as a relatively moderate space in terms of physical engagement.

Accentuation gesture: a third listening focuses on accentuation gestures that reveal fluctuations in *situational intensity.* The Largo is particularly animated during rush-hour periods and this gives rise to numerous occasions for intensification of experience: eruptions of dance music, nearby stationary traffic that suddenly starts to move again, thickening crowds, surrounding voices becoming more insistent, rumblings of street theatre, etc. All of these situations contribute to intensifying experience during the crossing and maintaining a high level of tension and stimulation. The voice tends to accompany this collective dynamic by switching to a hastier rhythm, its pitch rising and becoming more cheerful in character, thereby giving greater emphasis to what is being said. For example, the repetitive cries of street sellers sometimes turn into a mantra and the passer-by cannot help assimilating these and memorising their every inflection. In brief, the voice expresses not only the passer-by's physical engagement but the hold and tonality of the surrounding atmosphere. In a nutshell, Largo may be defined here as a space of high situational intensity.

'Tuning' gesture: a fourth listening reveals 'tuning' gestures that bring out diverse forms of *surrounding dynamics.* The most obvious example is, of course, the many times strollers vocally imitate music they have heard by reciting a lyrical passage or reproducing an especially catchy rhythm. The music that has been heard can generate an impetus that is very close to vocal imitation. However, there are also other phenomena in which the fit and timbre of the voice operate via transduction by expressing and embodying the dynamic of a sensory phenomenon from the ambient environment. For example, when the wind gets stronger, the passer-by remarks on this and pronounces "wiiiiiiiiind" in such a way as to make it last: he or she reproduces the type of weather that they experience through their voice. In other words, the mention of "the wind" is not merely a way of indicating its presence, it is also a means for those who experience it to express its existence from a temporal perspective (the elongated manner of pronouncing the word "wind" emulates the content of the gust of air itself). In other cases, the accelerated speech of the blind passer-by exacerbates the sudden acceleration of traffic or the plethora of nearby voices. Although Largo is criss-crossed by a multitude of ambient flows, each with its own dynamic (musical

tempo, pedestrian allure, passing currents of air, incessant rumour, etc.), it does not appear especially desynchronised. For our present purposes, we would define it as a rhythmical, highly resonant space.

So, what lessons should we draw from this attempt at listening to the ambient voice of Largo da Carioca? First, the sheer plasticity and power of vocal expression in a given situation is perfect for pointing up the atmospheric nuances of places. This gives rise to various different impregnations that colour behaviour and sensitise experiences; clear focuses that frame vocal expression and accompany the passer-by throughout the experiment. But here again, does this not point us towards an *ethnophony of ambiences*? In this regard, the various aforementioned phonic gestures relating to capturing attention, physical engagement, situational intensity and surrounding dynamics constitute a few of the many registers that participate *in situ* in sensitive experience. A singular listening channel needs to be developed, one that is highly sensitive to the tonalities of ambient situations and changes in the situated voice. On a concluding note, does the voice not act like an extraordinarily powerful resonator of the infinitesimal variations that comprise the urban soundscape?

Meri Kytö

Sound Diary Istanbul: Acoustemological Musings From The Field

Describing what one hears is probably one of the most labyrinth-
ine writing tasks for a researcher of auditory culture. How much
is enough? How thick should the description be? Although audio
recordings constitute viable 'notes-to-self' and can contribute
valuable acoustic archives to future generations, recordings alone
are insufficient to communicate the meanings that crisscross the
listening experience.

Listenings have dispositions; our attention shifts between sound
events. We adopt different listening modes in order to make sense of
our reactions, of the connotations, of the causalities, of the functions
and the semantics; we even empathetically feel out the intentions of
the source. Simultaneously, we are engaging the cognitive process of
imagining past sounds while casually listening to ongoing ones and
are making aesthetic judgements on the whole concoction.[1]

While I was collecting data for my study on sound culture in
Istanbul, I undertook regular investigations into the urban everyday, deploying writing to render the short listening experiences
as description in a way that would accompany my field recordings.
What follows are some selected examples.[2]

Sultanahmet, midday in April 2009. The Hagia Eirene (or Aya Irini)
church is located inside the walls of the Topkapı Palace. 1629 years
ago the church was getting ready for the First Council of Constanti-
nople. Now it is preparing for the opening gala of the international
poetry festival 'Siirİstanbul' and it is time for a sound check.

Chairs are being arranged, the PA is being tested, lighting rigs are
undergoing construction and are put through their paces. Planned for
the evening's performance is a reading of a poem that Nazim Hikmet

1. For more on listening modes see Tuuri, K. and Eerola, T. 2012. 'Formulating a Revised Taxonomy
for Modes of Listening'. *Journal of New Music Research*.
2. Visit http://sesligunluk.blogspot.com for the recordings

wrote to Taranta Babu in Rome, 1935. To give the performance a little more context, the beginning of the recital will be punctuated by the replay of a recording of Mussolini's 'Vincere e Vinceremo!' speech. The balance and timing needs to be sorted out. The vaults of the Byzantine church echo with the transphonic layers of history.

Thursday April 8th. The World Roma Day festivities have started in Balat at the shore of the Golden Horn (*Haliç*). The echoes of the *ezan* call to prayer make the festival pause for a few minutes but soon the undulating voices of the *müezzins* fade away and the festival's sound system is switched back on. The Çanakkale Lapseki Roma orchestra is warming up and doing a sound check. The clarinettist Hüsnü Şenlendirici strolls on the stage and soon the air fills with the sound of Roma music. The evening continues with more and more performers, the people dancing and enjoying themselves despite the cooling evening weather. Compelled to flee by decibel levels that have risen beyond high and are now at ear piercing, I escape to a nearby café I am able to enjoy the music again, now tempered by its journey through the building's walls.

On stage, the announcer thanks the local MP and city authorities for organising the event. There is a grim irony to this since the city authorities are set to bulldoze Balat and the neighbouring district of Fener in the very near future; the subsequent reconstruction may attract more tourists but to the detriment of local residents. These kind of gentrification projects are familiar to the former residents of Sulukule. Like Balat, Sulukulel was a Roma neighbourhood too.

Göztepe mosque, Sunday afternoon. I had the opportunity to parti-cipate in a ceremony that was arranged 40 days after the funeral a friend's relative. This prayer ceremony is called the *kırkı*, literally meaning the '40th'. It started right after the midday prayer.

The voice of the *imam* can be heard downstairs as the women enter the mosque from a small door at the back left of the building (*bayan cemaat girisi*). I cover my head with a scarf, take my shoes off and climb the wooden stairs to the second floor *haremlik*, a mezzanine with a small latticed balcony from which the women folk can get a glimpse of what is happening under the main dome in *selamlik*, the men's space. Some elderly women sit eyes closed on the balcony floor. They rock themselves gently to indicate religious concentration in listening to the *imam* after he starts the prayer with a strong melis-matic voice. After a while, the mezzanine's loudspeaker is turned on, it had been forgotten and was switched off when I entered the *haremlik*.

Soft carpet floors mellow the sounds of people walking calmly in their bare socks, greeting and hugging one another, some sobbing, some arranging their shoes in plastic bags and putting them on a shelf. The hum of the traffic seeps softly from the white curtained windows through which the occasional chirp of sparrows is heard.

Kabatas, Saturday afternoon. There was a small man inside the traffic light post. He was looking after us pedestrians very keenly. *"Lütfen bekleyin"* (Please wait). *"Simdi geçebilirsiniz"* (Now you may cross the road). *"Altı, bes, dört, üç, iki, bir"* (6, 5, 4, 3, 2, 1). "Bip–bip–bip–bip" (talking back to the cars that answered his instructions).

Eminönü ferry pier, 6 pm on a Tuesday. People have done their day's work and are running to catch the ferry to the Asian side, Kadıköy. In her book *Istanbullasmak*,[3] Meriç Öner writes about the *akbil*, a 'smart ticket', a small keychain-like magnet that can be used in Istanbul to pay fares at ferries, buses, metros, trains, the *tünel*, funicular, tram, you name it. According to Öner, there are all kind of things one can know about the person using the *akbil* simply through attentive listening to the electronic notes it creates. The A–E interval (first trip of the day), the B–A#–B–C# (s/he is a transfer passenger), the B–E–A#–B–E–A# (damn! Must get in the line… my *akbil* has dried up). All this *akbil*-powered human traffic turns the piers and ferry stops into auditoria of electric symphonies. Yet Öner points out that by far the

most intimidating sound of *akbil* is the silence that ensues when searching your pockets and your bag and just doesn't… now where is it!?

April at Emirgan Park, the Istanbul Tulip Festival has opened. There are tulips everywhere, a lot of them, in all shapes and colours. This is something you really have to see for yourself. However, the park's soundscape took on a different register to the visual environment. Colourful, yes, but not as serene. The park is very popular this time of the year. Among the glorious and lush tulips there were teenage

3. eds. P. Dervis, B. Tanju, and U. Tanyeli 2009. *Istanbullasmak. Olgular, sorunsallar, metaforlar* (Becoming Istanbul. Facts, problematics, metaphors). Istanbul: Garanti galeri.

girls skipping rope. *Bir–kii–üç, haydi!* (One, two, three! Come on!) The rope hitting the pavement is accompanied by giggles and laughter. In the background there are whistles of the park guards and babble from families having picnics, strolling around. One small boy is enjoying the thick, cool grass by rolling over it and patting it with his hands. He stops when he sees me, looking a bit shy with the sudden realisation that he's among others in a public park.

Returning to the observations that began this account, there may have been an opportunity to have rendered my descriptions more meticulous; thickening them with a deeper investigation into the echoes, resonance and rhythms of the sounds encountered in the Istanbul everyday. (And maybe I could have done this much better in my mother tongue, Finnish?) In many of the situations where I wrote my listening, I felt that it was more important to devote my energies to explaining the cultural and spatial context of my listening experience—even within the few words available—than it was to focus on the acoustic parameters of the sound events themselves. This is not to underestimate the dynamic complexities of those sound events—indeed, their description could stretch to pages and pages, whole essays addressing the single snap of that skipping rope. As such, finding the end to a description can be as fraught as choosing where to begin. Nonetheless, the responsibility involved in the verbal communication to another of how it was that you heard something (as sound event, as context) is such an important part of our inhabitation of the sensorial world that it can't be ignored. The commitment is to seek to learn better how to know and understand through listening, to write about what one hears.

Daniela Cascella

Listening, Reading, Writing: A Case Study

1. Listening

20 June 2010. I return today to the Protestant Cemetery in Rome. A
recurring place for thinking, and a favoured starting point for walks
between cypress trees and along the Aurelian walls, into via Appia
and the Roman aqueduct that appears intermittently along its path.
Today golden leaves gleam, dishevelled against a cloudy sky, as a
rainstorm has just cleared away. There is something raw and aching
about these clouds, although they are vanishing. The daisies and the
anemones blossom white and purple, a silent colourful counterpoint
to the soft hiss of the wind-brushed cypress trees. The sun lights up
the little tinsel vases by the marble slabs while above, on a branch,
the far-carrying, soft hoo-hoo of a hoopoe calls for more voices: the
embellished trill of chaffinch, the gentle purr of turtledove. All over,
the buzz of cicadas throws a maddening, enchanting veil on this
cerulean late afternoon.

I walk around and I see again, one by one, the tombs of Percy
Bysshe Shelley, of John Keats, of Antonio Gramsci. I walk around and I
begin to hear some words, some verses in fact. They arrive from a far
region of my memory, not from the landscape around me, yet their
sound and their pace are as clear to me as the rhythmic tinkle of the
little tinsel vases by the marble slabs, stirred by the breeze. They say:

> It isn't May-like, this impure air
> which darkens the foreigners' dark
> garden still more, then dazzles it
> with blinding sunlight... this foam-
> streaked sky above the ochre roof
> terraces which in vast semicircles veil
> Tiber's curves and Latium's cobalt
> mountains...

How can I make these words audible again? How can I bring together,
in one picture, the birdsongs against the moving branches, the buzz

of cicadas as it emerges out of the storm and into the birdsongs, the tinkle of the tinsel vases, and the humming of these verses as they hit my silent recollections?

2. Reading

The first time I visited the Protestant Cemetery in Rome, it was shut.

In typical Italian style, somebody had decided without announcing it, that it would only be open on a restricted schedule. It was in the spring of I-no-longer-remember-which year of the Nineties. After a long period of anticipation—to visit the tombs of adored poets Keats and Shelley!—I had to get back in my car and drive home, disappointed. The only thing that made up for my missed visit was a book, which I'd bought on the same day. It was titled *The Ashes of Gramsci*, it was a collection of poems written by Pier Paolo Pasolini in the Fifties, and it allowed me to see and hear the Protestant Cemetery for the first time, although in words: in *terza rima* verses, to be precise, chosen by Pasolini to give rhythm to his silent dialogue with Gramsci and with Shelley, in the setting of the cemetery on an "autumnal May".

That evening my visit to the cemetery took on the form of a Proustian anticipation, like those pages in *Swann's Way* where the writer imagines places and towns he never visited, just by reading their names. Instead of actually being there, I fashioned my visit upon the words of Pasolini. I imagined raising my eyes and seeing the "foam-streaked sky"; I could hear the sound of faded hammers from the nearby workshops in Testaccio; as a silent witness, I could hear Pasolini's imaginary conversation with the founder of the Italian Communist Party and with the Romantic poet, as he unravelled his struggle between social engagement and romantic tension; I could picture in my mind the "waxen light" curdle in the twilit neighbourhood and hear the "dim hum" of life encompassed in those verses; I could nearly feel the soft breeze, "dying with shivers of storms", graze my face.

Pasolini's verses are now ingrained in my experience of the place and every time I return there I can't prevent myself from hearing them, in the same manner as I couldn't prevent myself today from hearing the songs of hoopoe and chaffinch. I once learned those verses by heart, I hear them any time I return.

By heart I hear.

I go back to my copy of *The Ashes of Gramsci*. "The foreigners' dark garden", "desperate vibrations scrape the silence" and "silent,

humid, fruitless" are verses I underlined on every subsequent visit
to the cemetery, accompanied by that book. On its back pages I
once made a note of the assonant line "thro' the thick throbbings of
her trembling throat" recalled from another poem, *The Nightingale*
by Algernon Charles Swinburne. I made a note of it the first time I
heard a nightingale, on exiting the cemetery early one evening. I
liked the way the song of the nightingale merged with the buzz of
cicadas—a sound that fills many summer days and evenings in Rome.
I then thought of the myth of the birth of cicadas, narrated by Plato
in *Phaedrus*: of men who existed before the Muses, and who died
from the pleasure of listening to their song. They were eventually
transformed into cicadas, and granted to sing for eternity. I have
always been inclined to draw a parallel between this myth and the
delirious quality of listening: the disclosure of sound within the
exhilarating experience of listening, and within every account of
such experience in words.

As I set out to write of my repeated listening moments in the
Protestant Cemetery through the filter of Pasolini's verses and of my
memories, what I am to outline cannot be but a layered construction
of all the thoughts and words and sounds that have been with me
on every visit through the years, and hit my every return—my every
now, with its load of thens crashing on it. There is no claim for
authenticity or immediacy in the following picture. It doesn't matter
what is real and what is fake in its repeating patterns. I shift the
glance, and the ear, to its texture, woven in such a hybrid operation.
Rather than interrogating the provenance and aim of this scene,
I'd lose myself in the spinning vortex of recalled, reinvented and
revisited images, sounds and words. I no longer know what was real
and what I imagined, what I heard and what I made myself believe
I was hearing. I construct a place, I channel a presence, as a frayed
palimpsest of notated experiences, anticipations, recollections.

3. Writing

Golden leaves gleam, dishevelled against a cloudy sky. There is still
something raw and aching about these clouds, although they are
vanishing. The entire scene seems covered by a soaked damp veil.
Above and below and in the distance and in the forefront, everything
is still wet with rain, but starts shimmering again.

Golden leaves gleam, dishevelled against a cloudy sky. Desperate
vibrations scrape the silence.

Where lies the spirit of this place? Surely it is rooted within its history, in the shape of these trees, and in stories passed on from people to people. It also lies in the flora and the fauna, in the weather, and in the seasons. In a specific season, at a specific time, the spirit of this place unveils to me, as I hear and uncover nuances in its sounds, and dig into its stories and into the words inscribed in it.

Desperate vibrations against a cerulean cloudy sky.

For some time, soon after the storm, everything seems quiet. Silence, humid, fruitless. All the sounds seem to be sleeping, or afraid to break out. Then they reappear: the rhythmic tinkle of the little tinsel vases by the marble slabs, stirred by the breeze, as tiny needles weaving a fabric of stillness, now open to the arabesques of the song of hoopoe, chaffinch, turtledove. *Upupa epops*, *Fringilla coelebs*, *Streptopelia turtur.*

I can hear a voice, or it is the wind blowing muffled verses across the branches?

> *It isn't May-like, this impure air*
> *which darkens the foreigner's dark*
> *garden still more...*

At twilight, the nightingale will darken this foreigners' dark garden, "thro' the thick throbbings of her trembling throat".

Golden leaves gleam, dishevelled against a cloudy sky.

Enchanted and enchained by the pleasure of a song, soon the cicadas will start buzzing again.

Barry Blesser & Linda-Ruth Salter

Hearing Events in Space

The Functional Role of Hearing

While *Homo sapiens* eventually expanded the mammalian auditory system for understanding speech and enjoying music, the auditory system originally was a reliable way for sensing dynamic events. A sonic event is some (man-made or natural) activity that produces a sudden impact or periodic vibrations, which then produce sound waves that propagate through the environment. Sound transports the event into the listener's consciousness. The soundscape is therefore an *eventscape*. Because hearing is always active without 'earlids', listeners are involuntarily connected to those events that are audible. For example, an unexpected thump from the roof immediately catches our attention because sound is an early warning system.

Aural Boundaries are Experiential

From the perspective of listeners, a sonic event that can be heard is located within their *acoustic horizon*. Beyond this acoustic horizon, sound sources are inaudible, as if they did not exist. In the complementary view centred at the sound source, an *acoustic arena* is that area within which a particular sonic event can be heard by the inhabitants of the arena. Acoustic horizons and acoustic arenas define invisible boundaries based on aural experience rather than on tangible physical surfaces; they are functional partitions of a space.

How we experience the eventscape strongly influences our behaviour. Consider two professional colleagues at a busy restaurant who are discussing a business project. Given their relationship, they have a preferred personal distance, which might be 1 metre. If a high level of background noise produces a small acoustic horizon, conversation is not possible at this distance. These colleagues have awkward choices: move closer to create an inappropriate intimate social distance, thus including each other in the acoustic arena of their normal voices; shout to expand their acoustic horizon; or remain silent without conversing. Emotional stress results when the acoustic arena does not match the appropriate social distance.

There have always been conflicts about who 'owns' the eventscape in urban environments, and these conflicts were seldom resolved by legal regulations. In the picture below, Hogarth depicts conflict between a musician in the parlour of his private home and urbanites whose home is the street. From a visual perspective, there are two distinct spaces—street and parlour; but from an aural perspective, the open window creates a single acoustic arena as a shared resource.

In the 21st century, combat over ownership of the acoustic arena has become more ubiquitous. Advertisers use televisions in the public areas of airports to insert monetized messages into the heads of those waiting for their flights. As a reaction, individuals often adopt a defensive strategy, using headphones linked to portable sound devices in order to suppress the external eventscape and substitute their own eventscape.

Physical spaces can have unexpected shapes and sizes such that the experience of visual and aural spaces diverges. For example, large spaces with domed ceilings and circular walls can produce acoustic arenas called 'whispering galleries', where the sound from one location is focused at a physically distant location; two widely separated visual regions are combined into a single acoustic arena. Thus, two people standing at opposite corners in the dining concourse of the Grand Central Station in New York can hear each

William Hogarth 'The Enraged Musician', 1741
(Courtesy of Graphic Arts Collection, Princeton University)

other as if they were standing in close proximity. In this case, the two senses—vision and hearing—rather than reinforcing a consistent spatial experience, produce quite different spaces. Eventscapes and objectscapes can be experienced in contradictory ways.

Modern technology provides us with the means for creating inconsistent eventscapes and objectscapes. Electronically amplified excessively loud music at a rock concert allows the hearer to be transported to a musical eventscape while remaining in the physical objectscape of the seating area. Teleconferencing allows physically distant objectscapes to be fused into a single eventscape; individuals separated by large distances can aurally co-exist within the same acoustic arena. Cell phones allow unrelated eventscapes to be superimposed onto each other. Consider an individual talking on a cell phone while travelling in a car; he is in the eventscape of traffic on a busy road, and simultaneously in the eventscape of his conversation partner who is in a business meeting. The talker can perceptually switch between eventscapes without physically moving. What you see is not necessarily where you are.

Sonic Events and Acoustic Space

The auditory system can perceive objects and geometries by the way that it interprets ambient reflected sound. A listener can hear the way in which physical attributes of the environment change sound. We can hear a low hanging ceiling or nearby wall because the low frequencies are boosted near those surfaces. We can hear an open door, the vast volume of a cavern or cathedral, wood surfaces, the depth of a well, and the openness of a beach. In such cases, we hear properties of the objectscape because sonic events illuminate objects and geometries.

Everyone can learn to hear objects and geometries of the environment, but most people never attend to this aspect of hearing. Some blind individuals choose to invest in this skill. Ray Charles, the world famous jazz musician, describes how he learned to navigate entirely with his hearing, never using a cane or seeing-eye dog. The way in which objects and geometries modify sonic events allows listeners to 'visualise' the environment, which produced the change in the sonic event. Our auditory awareness of objectscapes augments our aural experience of eventscapes.

Listeners never hear the original sonic event as it was created at the source. As sound waves propagate from the source to the listener, they are always changed during the transport process by the physical acoustics of the environment. The reflections from side walls in a concert hall add aural mass to musical events. A room with plush carpets and upholstered chairs transforms a harsh sonic event, such as a breaking glass, into a mellow event. The notes of a musical instrument are elongated by the reverberation of a concert hall. The audience never hears a 'pure' musical instrument. The physical properties of the environment always modify the events in an eventscape; each space creates a unique modification of these events.

There is a dual relationship between sonic events and spatial acoustics. On the one hand, a sonic event illuminates objects in a space, such as sensing a wall by the echo that it produces. On the other hand, spatial acoustics change the perception of sonic events, such as music performed in a concert hall. We hear objects and geometries illuminated by sonic events, and we hear sonic events that have been changed by objects and geometries.

A high quality concert hall exemplifies the complex relationship between sonic events and the physical environment. A musical performance in an open meadow is not experienced in a way that is comparable to a performance in a concert hall. In an enclosed space, the early reflections from the side walls and ceiling change music notes by giving them more aural mass, larger apparent size, and stronger intimacy. Musical events originating on the stage are changed by the enclosing envelope of the concert hall.

At the same time, long reverberation envelops the audience in a sea of sound that is not perceived as a sonic event originating from the stage. Cathedrals, with their extremely long enveloping reverberation, allow inhabitants to hear the enormous volume of the space and the hardness of the surfaces regardless of what sonic events are illuminating that volume.

Summary and Conclusions

We inhabit eventscapes where dynamic sonic events, modified by the static acoustics of the space, are transported to listeners. Eventscapes are described by the virtual boundaries of acoustic horizons and acoustic arenas. Combat over control of the acoustic arena has occurred throughout the ages. Individuals have complex cognitive strategies for determining how eventscapes are controlled and integrated into their daily lives. These strategies depend upon individuals' unique personal choices, cultural standards, and the state of technology.

Steve Rowell

Peaks and Nulls: Beneath the Supersonic Airspace Above the Mojave Desert

When entering the space of a California desert for the first time, people are often struck by the silence and stillness of the air, especially in the summer months when radiant heat from all directions seems to compress time. The winters are less silent: windstorms blow drift-snow from mountains miles away for weeks on end and rain can come in violent bursts, called 'gully washers', scouring out low-lying areas, sweeping the desert floor barren once again. The dynamics of climate and nature, and the effects on the acoustic qualities of the desert are surprisingly varied. Like anywhere else, there is a daily rhythm despite all of these variances. Birds provide an acoustic timescale with their waking, feeding, sleeping, and mating routines. They also react to inclement weather and manmade sounds, becoming either more excitable or completely silent during these interruptions. Passing cars near highways and off-road vehicles virtually everywhere else, commercial jetliners above and distant trains all add to this presence, or 'fieldtone', of the open desert. One particular swath of the California Mojave desert has another element: something unique in its signature and source, frequency and impact: the sonic boom. Extremely rare in many places on Earth—a spectacle that is one of the loudest sounds we humans can create short of a nuclear explosion—it happens on an almost daily basis here, originating from a restricted military airspace called the R–2508 Special Use Airspace Complex. It is a vast void above some of the most uninhabitable desert terrain in America, situated between Los Angeles and Las Vegas, covering all of Death Valley and a few dozen other sun-blasted valleys and dry lakes equally daunting to the inexperienced traveller. It was in one of these forbidding places, in 2005, where I started a project entitled the *Sonic Boom Archive*.

Sonic booms are the audible effects of shock waves caused by matter moving faster than the speed of sound—approximately 761 mph at sea level at 59°F (1,224 kph at 15°C)—through the atmosphere. In this case, the types of 'matter' are various supersonic military aircraft that may include the US Air Force F-16, F/A-18, F-22, and F-35 fighter jets as well as NASA's F-5A and F-15B Shaped Sonic Boom Demonstrator jets. These otherwise exotic aircraft are common to the airspace above the Mojave Desert.

Over the course of 18 months, from 2005-2007, I recorded all of the sonic boom events that occurred as a result of this regular, almost routine shattering of the sound barrier. The equipment array installed was calibrated to autonomously monitor and record any sound above an established decibel threshold, filtering out long moments of (perceived) silence and/or low volume sounds, natural and man-made. The result was a reverse noise gate that allowed only abrupt and loud sounds to be recorded, thereby capturing the elusive sonic boom-scape of this singularly militarised, supersonic airspace, the largest and most active of its kind in the world. In order to truly capture these fleeting percussive sounds (lasting only milliseconds), I used a software-based audio buffer that recorded the time before and after the booms. This provided for a parallel archive to take form: an incidental soundtrack of the ambient desert. The Sonic Boom Archive recordings themselves amount to hundreds of sonic booms, some distant and almost imperceptible, while others were so loud they caused the metal roof of the building inside which the equipment array was installed to reverberate from the severe air pressure impact, ringing and vibrating like an enormous resonant diaphragm, an aluminum membrane responding to the tactile force of repeating shock-waves.

The shock-wave of a sonic boom has a characteristic 'overpressure profile'; figures of which fill page after page of reports that have been generated by NASA since the early 1960s when research on this new phenomenon began. The 'N-wave', as it's called, has two peaks, one positive and one negative, representing, first, the pressure generated by the nose of the aircraft, as it breaks the sound barrier, and second, the pressure returning to normal, just behind the tail of the aircraft. This wave of pressure is projected away from the aircraft in all directions, in a cone, behind the aircraft, which is actually outrunning the conical wave, ahead of the pressure (and sound) it generates. When the cone strikes the ground, it generates a form, called a 'boom carpet' which is typically 20-30 miles wide. The size of this shock-wave and the intensity of the boom depends more on the mass of the object than its speed. Because of this N-wave, a noticeable double boom sound is the result. Two peaks separated by a split-second. This brief moment in time, between the sounds—this null space—is the silence of the supersonic plane itself. In effect, the plane has achieved a contradictory state of simultaneous being and non-being, at least to our ears. If applied to the pilot of the craft, the old riddle "If a tree falls in a forest…" becomes even more puzzling. Indeed, when US Air Force pilots began setting records of super and hyper sonic speeds, Mach 1.0, 2.0, even 3.0 and higher, in the late 1950s, writers of popular fiction extrapolated wildly. Many radio plays, comic books, and TV programs imagined the pilot and craft entering alternate realities, sometimes never to return.

The airspace above the equipment array is known as the R–2508 Special Use Airspace Complex and is the most effectively integrated Special Use Airspace in the National Airspace System, indeed it is the most active peacetime military airspace in the world. It is managed by a group representing the complex's three primary user organizations—the Naval Air Warfare Center Weapons Division at China Lake, the Air Force Flight Test Center at Edwards Air Force Base, and the National Training Center at Fort Irwin. It provides the largest single area of overland Special Use Airspace within the United States. The complex includes the R–2515 High Altitude Supersonic Corridor (directly overhead the equipment array) and the Black Mountain Supersonic Corridor beginning just a few miles north of the equipment array. The public relations division at Edwards Air Force Base describes the R–2508 and R–2515 as airspaces capable of almost anything and that have "intense test and test support traffic. Operations may include live bombings and airdrops… lifting body experiments (like the Space Shuttle), all imaginable types of flight testing to include supersonic flight on a daily basis, 4 spin areas, and flight training for the USAF Test Pilot School. This area is active at all times." The Air Force does not provide schedules of supersonic training and testing to members of the public, including those residents living beneath the R–2508.

On the ground, beneath this hyper-regulated and restricted airspace is the town of Hinkley, one of hundreds of desert communities that have seen better days. It sits between Interstate 15—which carries Angelenos to and from the casinos of Vegas—and the empty slab of Harper Dry Lake from where Howard Hughes once flew his experimental (and subsonic) airplanes. Just north of Hinkley, past a high school, towards a forbidding horizon of dark mountains called The Black Mountain range lies a small fenced compound behind a fading white sign. This is the Center for Land Use Interpretation's Desert Research Station. It is here, directly beneath the most active portion of the supersonic corridor, that the Sonic Boom Archive project was initiated. This small collection of buildings with an interpretive trail is the site where the CLUI is now planning to open another artist residency program, similar to the original program in Wendover, UT. However, as a reaction to the Sonic Boom Archive and other experimental audio-based events and projects that have occurred since, this residency program will focus on sound-based work.

More information is available from www.steverowell.com/sba

Ross Brown

The Human Auditorium

Auditoria are not constructed from stone or wood alone;
aurality is not merely auditory.

1.

Postsomethingly, I am cycling through south London in 2011, listening
to a recording on my iPod. I am up close and personal with the London
permadrone, negotiating its component vrooms, blasts and hisses. The
headphones I am wearing let me hear them. Those which are important
inform and divert my course, while the others dissolve into the noise/
silence that is unwittingly heard; the background insignificance of
neglected data. I am navigating this forest of noise, and yet here I am
in an intimate listening space, reading complicated audio-literature
and following musical or verbal discourses that speak in the vicinity
of the listening and reflexively thinking *me*, located behind my eyes
and between my ears. These headphones; this head: they're bigger on
the inside. I'm in an energised, portable capsule of aural immediacy,
at whose centre both *logos* and *phonos* sound in a think-space that
has an up, a down, a back, a front; the inner surface of whose sphere
is a diorama of urban noise-scenery that vies for and fragments my
attention with its perpetually fleeting panorama of moment. This head-
bubble, within which I listen and hear, is engaged by a programme and
distracted from it by circumstance; *this* is the auditorium within which
I do all my listening these days. I am a subject of the personal audio
age of constant intermedial possibility and even when I am not literally
negotiating the hurly-burly of the daily journey, *this* is the auditorium
within which I have learned and practice my audience technique.
   Now I am sat in a dark room, with other static, listening bodies lined
up in rows over *here*. We are watching a lit stage, over *there*, on which
someone is speaking some lines. In theory it is like a *camera obscura*,
a dark and silent space within which, from a certain critical distance,
we critically gaze upon and listen into a projection of reality. Except
it is not a dark and silent space; it is full of noise, both mundanely
native, and exotically imagined. And even here and now, with naked,
headphone-free ears, amidst the conventional presumption of presence,

liveness and shared experience, I feel disconnected, from the room, from the others; still in my own listening booth; deranged by my in-ear, in-car, surround-sound training; by the ever-present environmental possibility of the acousmatically strange, the anachronistic, the transient or the otherwise out-of-place. This is not an immersion in sound but in my sonic self. I am listening, but the location of the sound I am hearing is in *here*. Or maybe it is an argument between *here* and *there* (my centre-stage here in my head; the actor's centre-stage there). The argument resonates, reverberates and echoes within these walls and the conventions and noises of this room, but the auditorium is mine; is me.

2.

Romantically, I am taking a recreational walk through forest glades south of London in the early nineteenth-century, along the route where the bounds of Lambeth and Croydon are annually beaten into the aural memories of parish choirboys. I carry a Claude Glass—would that there were an auditory equivalent. By M. De Loutherbourg's book of engravings, *The Picturesque Scenery of Great Britain*, and particularly by his Eidophusikon sounding picture show, which, as Mr Pyne has commented, proposes a *picturesque of sound*, I am instructed to listen to the wind in the trees and the torrent of the Effra stream, which while hardly the sublimely thunderous waterfall De Loutherbourg once depicted in his Drury Lane pantomime *The Wonders of Derbyshire*, still gushes from the ornamental lake at Norwood House with a *profundo* power. By the lake, Mrs Nesbitt has positioned an Aeolian harp, which from time to time catches the wind and produces an undulating drone, like the sustain and decay of a chord, but without the rhetorical flourish of a human musician's attack. It dies away sadly, as if from the sky, and I am reminded of Faust waking in the ethereal sonic glow of Aeolian harps at the commencement of the second part of Goethe's play. Mr Coleridge recently suggested that the automatic music of these popular gadgets reveals, without the intervention of human art, "a light in sound, a sound-like power in light" (by which he means some universal force or metaphysical truth which Goethe, Mesmer, Hartley *et al.* propose not as idealism, figuration or occultism, but science). No longer, then, is the *musica* of Boethius and the quadrivium a divine symmetry *beyond* experience; it is a field of energy, in which I am immersed and which animates me. As an auditorium, this gushing of water and the profound breeze that causes trees, harp strings and nervous system to quiver with sound—*this* forest, whether I stand in it, or it in me—is a realm where I am subject only to my senses and the world with which they connect me.

3.

Classically, I attend an amphitheatre built into a Greek hillside, late 5th century BC.

I no longer hear the incessant cicadas—their inescapable rhythm, I suppose, no more than a texture behind me and to the sides. They reflect a little from the front of the *skena frons* before me, but they have no significance down there in the playing area, where only man-made noises have meaning in a scheme of universal themes and the educating words of the poet. Behind it, as the hill slopes downwards towards the sea, there is blue sonic yonder within which only the occasional distant events sound; a bird (maybe an owl or a heron); a goat. The warm breeze comes and goes, in the olive branches and against my skin, and the sound undulates slightly with each occasional zephyr. Sound seems implicated in the wafting heat and smells that appear subtly to emanate from hillside itself. This is the same vaporous emanation to which the oracles, perched on their tripods, listen by breathing it in through their vaginas and then broadcasting it onwards as the babble within which the male priests hear verbal prophecy. We call it *aura,* because it is of *au*, the air or atmosphere. Sound; heat; smell; breeze—all the ways in which this place reaches me through my skin—these are aural phenomena. Hearing; smell; touch—these are senses of atmosphere. The auditorium is full and there is something else in the air—the feel of a crowd listening, the fragility of its attention; the threat of its distraction; the possibility of its coughing, laughing, whispering or leaving. The audience's flesh and clothing absorb sound even as they give-off *aura*, and by design there is no architectural resonance or reverberation in this stone-built amphitheatre. Words carry straight and true to ears that line a semi-spherical auditorium that itself is not unlike an ear hewn into the hillside. Occasionally drums or manufactured thunder sound, roomily, from somewhere in the wooden building behind the scene. But this amphitheatre is a temple of ideas, a place for listening to speech, not wallowing in voice. The resonant gathering together of vowels into that supernatural tonal energy that seems to exceed itself in the caves where ancestors are honoured, and which inspires a kind of trance in those who practice such rituals; the death-defying prolongation of sounds by reverberation—these effects obscure clarity and speak to the body rather than the mind. Only a reference to such primitive sonic practices is allowed in this civic theatre, in the constrained dance, the raucous aulos pipes and the stylised wails of female mourning. Some of the chorus have wooden masks of a special type which project such intonations so that they may faintly resonate in large brass jars set around the auditorium, causing the auditorium quietly to ring from time-to-time at certain preordained pitches. Nothing uncontrolled has meaning: the contained resonance; the drums; the pipes; the rhythmic chanting; the arrhythmic moments of hullabaloo: all are programmed; performed; have function; meant to mean something. The incidental cicadas; goat; bird—they are outside; not part of the theatre until the drama ends.

Jérôme Joy

Auditoria & Audiences— 'Shakkei'—借 景 and the Out in the Open Listening Experience

The reason why music becomes a series of sound expanses—besides explanations related to the search for unusual acoustics and unexpected possibilities of sound transmissions that both arrive with the wider frame enabled by extended outdoor spaces—relates to the opportunity to open up a mix of ambience and place. This 'opening up' is also a 'musical transformation'—synchronous and a-synchronous—of the social space. In other words, music opens up an attentive and focused attitude, at once collective and singular, that intensifies our (mutual and individual) consciousness through the listening to what comes (in all its fortuitous flows) and the music is thus created, fabricated and composed; a music that we designate as such.

We could call this opened mix of ambience and place, this musi-calisation of social space, an 'audiosphere'. This audiosphere, in the context of contemporary listening practices and the increasingly sophisticated systems available for diffusion, has the distinction today in that it becomes mediated by sound transportation systems across to other remote acoustic spaces. This audiosphere is neither antagonistic nor complementary to the music aimed for concert houses (such as *Musikhaus* or *Kammermusik*). Both of these approaches diffuse various facets of the real (they are, after all, '*passeurs de réels*') and are linked to diverse listening experiences. Experiences that run a continuum from a directed listening—for which every acoustic event demands attention ('panacousticon') —to another, less directed form of listening, one that we must direct and adapt ourselves, and which remains in all likelihood partial and wandering, yet which nevertheless has the capacity to profoundly alter our perception of our environments and, ultimately, the world itself.

The reason why I devote myself today to exploring the conditions of an extended music, through concerts and performances that frequently oscillate between improvisation and composition, between strategies of minimum and maximum saturation of acoustic spaces ('merging into the surroundings'), by deploying instrumental, electronic and networked music (this latter term can also be understood to encompass both 'telemusic' and musical sonification) is because this is how it seems to me that music can work to manufacture listening experiences. Only through such a complex assemblage can the different dimensions of distance listening be invoked. For me, it is critically imperative that this manufacturing of the listening experience be investigated, precisely in order to question our surroundings. This process of manufacturing—effectively the establishment of an *auditorium*—collaborates with the environment and experiments with acoustic expanses; it modifies, to repeat, our ways of perceiving and enables us to participate, evaluate and modulate together the very listening experience that is being constructed.

These constructions are able to simultaneously alter our participation as listeners and our perception of what music is made of, between what it is to receive those played sounds and what it is that constitutes the played sounds themselves. Participation in these audiospheres is an art of roaming and of interpreting. An auditorium is a space, constituted itself by various spaces (imaginary, fictive, apparent, suggested) involving different scales and routes, depths and shades, that could be compared to an architecture and to a landscape.

To play sounds while wandering across different spaces (and fluxes) involves the transmitted sounds successively lighting up echoing acoustics. Our wandering follows the furrow and 'groove', without having to record or read a preliminary sound. It creates the impression of audio filtering as distances between transmission and reception increase and decrease, as sounds leave and then return from the surfaces of the spaces reverberated and reflected. In some respects, this is reminiscent of the practice of ambulatory lighting as it stimulates and explores acoustic spaces through the soundscape. What is *already there* becomes real through our wandering movement and the distances we establish between things. The interpretation of these perceptible spaces, either occasionally or as something more regular, involves seizing the opportunity of the moment and the place, making what is *already there* manifest through its multiple fragments and variations, as if they were so many coloured and tinted planes and volumes. These kinds of perception profoundly and permanently alter the topography: the road and the landscape are more complex than they seemed to be at first. At the same time, we both lose our way and discover new landmarks.

To play instrumental or electronic music out in the open and to move around (and we could extend the notion to incorporate the mobile listening and portable music delivered through, for example, permeable headphones from podcasting, iPods or Walkmen) is to see the auditorium being progressively manufactured as the piece is played. The auditorium—the place: auricle, horn and membrane— becomes defined as the musicians move and progressively spread themselves in the space, like electrons or in clusters. This movement and spreading creates a powerful impulse; the listeners divide themselves in the manner of a choir (from the Greek term, *choros*), fortuitously creating a *chôra*, which for Plato meant the 'space' where form materialised but which here means a temporary establishment of the space. The listeners navigate their listening in relation to the performers' instruments responding to each other by phrases and through the echoing between points in the open space. Distances vary constantly between the instrumentalists themselves, and between the audience. Yet, instead of tearing apart the music and dissolving it into whatever constitutes the current acoustic background (such as the rush of the waves and the roar of the wind, or the sounds of the urban everyday), the aim is to create paths and expanses in sound that develop a more balanced relationship to the surrounding environment. These movements create an ensemble in the meaning of 'playing music together' as the performers and the listeners adjust to each other from a distance. This parallels the ways that the performers encounter unity and harmony between each other through calibrating their unique music to its fate as it is acted on acoustically by the environment with all its structural characteristics.

Let us set the scene.

This art of manufacturing the space of remote listening encounters, by analogy, another art: *shakkei*. In Japanese tradition, *shakkei* (which literally means 'borrowed scenery') refers to the subtle practice of gardening considered as a technique of perception, construction and interpretation of reality (and of collaboration with the exterior world). It corresponds to what is called *mitate* ('see like') and, if taken into the acoustic field could be translated as *ototate* (a term surprisingly close to that of *Oto date*, which designates the listening station works of Akio Suzuki).

Thinking of distance listening / extended music in relation to *shakkei* allows us to become aware of how the multiple successive planes integrates within a single perspective; it reminds us of the conscious decision involved in placing an item (such as, for the gardener, a plant) in a relationship between the foreground and a remote background. The plant in front of you is placed in a composed layout: the organised bed nearby, and a mountain far away, for example. We suggest that extended music and distance listening serve as 'clutches' for such situations: through collaborating and borrowing from the distance, experimenting with expanses and modulating our own listening(s).

Selected references

Schütz, Alfred. 1951. 'Making Music Together: a Study on Social Relationship' in Schütz, A. 1964, *Collected Papers 1*, Den Haag, Martinus Nijhoff, pp.159–178.

Gould, Glenn. 1966. 'The Prospects of Recording', in Page, Tim (ed.). *The Glenn Gould Reader*. London: Vintage Books, 1993.

Ingold, Tim. 2000. *The perception of the environment: essays on livelihood, dwelling and skill*. London: Routledge.

Translation from French by Celine Cruickshanks and by the author; revised by Angus Carlyle.

Contributors

David Rothenberg is the author of *Why Birds Sing*, published in many languages and also turned into a BBC television documentary. Rothenberg has also written *Sudden Music*, *Always the Mountains*, and *Thousand Mile Song*, about making music live with whales. Rothenberg has released seven CDs under his own name, including *On the Cliffs of the Heart*, named one of the top ten CDs by *Jazziz* Magazine in 1995. His latest book is *Survival of the Beautiful*, on aesthetics in evolution. His first CD on ECM Records, with pianist Marilyn Crispell, *One Dark Night I Left My Silent House*, was released in 2010. Rothenberg is professor of philosophy and music at the New Jersey Institute of Technology.

Penny McCall Howard has a PhD in anthropology from the University of Aberdeen. She previously worked as crew and a skipper on passenger vessels in the United States and is presently employed as a maritime trade union researcher. Her academic research develops a labour-centered approach to human-environment and human-machine relations and shows how the ecology of places, the techniques people practise, and the subjectivities they enact are significantly affected by market pressures and class relations.

Gianni Pavan is Professor of Bioacoustics and Terrestrial and Marine Bioacoustics at the University of Pavia, Italy. He is President of the Centro Interdisciplinare di Bioacustica e Ricerche Ambientali which he co-founded in 1989 to develop advanced bioacoustic research based on digital techniques. His main research interests are on marine mammal acoustics, the impact of underwater noise on marine mammals, marine and terrestrial soundscapes, and acoustic ecology. He has cooperated with ONR, NATO, EDA, WHOI, IT Navy, INFN, INGV and other institutions worldwide to study and protect marine mammals. www.unipv.it/cibra mammiferimarini.unipv.it

Andrew Whitehouse is a birder and anthropologist, who teaches at the University of Aberdeen. His research has included fieldwork in Islay, Scotland, where he investigated the relations between nature conservation and the local community. More recently he has explored the human relations with bird sounds through the 'Listening to Birds' project, funded by the Arts and Humanities Research Council. This research examined such varied aspects of listening as recording and imitation, the skill of identifying sounds and their significance in sensing place, time and season. He is co-editor of the volume *Landscapes Beyond Land*, published by Berghahn in 2012.

Jean-Paul Thibaud, sociologist and urban planner, is a CNRS Senior Researcher at Cresson (Centre de Recherche sur l'Espace Sonore et l'Environnement Urbain / Research Center on Sonic Space and the Urban Environment). His field of research is related to the theory of urban ambiences, ordinary perception in the urban environment and the sensory culture and ethnography of public places, and he has published extensively on those topics. He is the scientific coordinator of the International Ambiances Network and the co-organiser of the 2nd International Congress on Ambiances (Montreal, 2012). www.ambiances.net

Meri Kyto is an ethnomusicologist and a cultural researcher finishing her PhD on articulations of private and public acoustic spaces in urban environments. Her publications tackle the sound cultures of Finland and Turkey on topics such as apartment acoustemology, acoustic communities of football fans and sonic representations of Istanbul in cinema. She has edited three books on soundscape research including *Acoustic Environments in Change* (2009) and has been active in the Finnish Society for Acoustic Ecology and its various soundscape projects from 1999.

Daniela Cascella is an Italian writer based in London. Her research explores Writing Sound in connection to landscape and memory, and fictional tropes in criticism. Her new book *En abîme: Listening, Reading, Writing. An Archival Fiction* was published by Zero Books in November 2012. She holds an MFA in Art Writing from Goldsmiths, University of London. Before moving to the UK she worked in Italy as a journalist and curator specialising in sound art, and was contributing editor of Italy's leading music magazine *Blow Up*. Her essays have been published in anthologies and catalogues internationally; her articles and reviews have appeared in *Organised Sound*, *MusicWorks*, *The Wire* and *frieze.com*.
www.danielacascella.com
enabime.wordpress.com

Dr. Blesser received his S.B, S.M, and Ph.D. from MIT in 1964, 1965 and 1969 specializing in communications, and was an Associate Professor for 9 years. Since leaving MIT in 1978, he has pursued a consulting career. He is considered one of the grandfathers of the digital audio revolution, having developed the first commercial digital reverberation system in 1976. In 2007, MIT Press published his first book, *Spaces Speak, Are You Listening? Experiencing Aural Architecture*, which he wrote with his co-author (and wife) Dr. Linda Salter. As independent scholars for the last five years, they have focused on the phenomenology of hearing space, auditory spatial awareness, analysis of eventscapes, aural architecture, and the language of sound and space.

Dr. Linda-Ruth Salter was a pioneer in crossing discipline boundaries when she obtained a Ph.D. degree in Interdisciplinary Studies from Boston University in 1983. Her doctoral dissertation examined the nature of sacred space in secular societies. Dr. Salter was a lecturer in the Urban Studies Program at Boston University, and served as Associate Professor in the Humanities and Social Sciences at New England Institute. She has been providing consulting services in planning for effective built environments in public housing, educational and business spaces. Her present research interests explore the aural experience of place, fusing symbolism, art and the phenomenon of environmental perception.

Steve Rowell is an artist, researcher, and Program Manager at the Center for Land Use Interpretation (CLUI). Being somewhat uprooted and working between Los Angeles, Washington DC, and Berlin, he also collaborates with SIMPARCH in Chicago and Cincinnati and The Office of Experiments in London.
www.steverowell.com
www.clui.org

Ross Brown studied as a painter but since the mid-1980s has worked as a composer, musician, technician, sound designer, academic and writer. He is Dean of Studies at Central School of Speech and Drama, University of London, where he has established sound as a core dramaturgical and scenographic consideration of theatre, as well as a specialist technical art. His research develops discursive frameworks for practice-as-research and theories of theatre sound, noise and aurality that bridge the fields of drama, theatre, sound studies and sonic arts practices. He lives in South London and holds the UK's only Chair in Theatre Sound.

Jérôme Joy is a French composer and musician working in instrumental, live electronic and electro acoustic music, and network music. He is currently engaged in a PhD in audio art and experimental music at Laval University (Quebec). Since 2004 he has been a Research Director (with Peter Sinclair) of the research group Locus Sonus Audio in Art and is a tenured Professor of Sound Arts at the National School of Arts Bourges (F). Recent projects and research include 'NMSAT Networked Music & SoundArt Timeline'; JOKTTJJEG (a noise quartet with Julien Ottavi, Kasper T. Toeplitz and Emmanuelle Gibello); 'Geographies Variables' a research residency at UQAM Montreal and 'Klar' for clarinets and live-electronics.
jeromejoy.org

Introduction by Angus Carlyle

Listening Devices

In Freud's *Civilisation and Its Discontents* there is a particular passage which—for me at least—erupts like a fascinating pustule on an otherwise unblemished expanse of skin. "Man has, as it were, become a kind of prosthetic God. When he puts on all his auxiliary organs he is truly magnificent; but those organs have not grown on to him and they still give him much trouble at times." In part, Freud is rehearsing the same theatre of devices and senses that Marshall McLuhan later developed into his theoretical drama where media extend our ostensibly innate carnal capacities and these extensions "whether of skin, hand, or foot, [affect] the whole psychic and social complex". Although McLuhan has his own eruptions of strangeness—such as his declaration that "we have extended our central nervous system in a global embrace, abolishing both space and time as far as our planet is concerned"—his extensions seem more stable in their mobilization of a basic sensorial integrity into which equally coherent devices find themselves plugged. With Freud, the strangeness endures in the identification of the trouble in the process of prosthesis (the "discontents" in the title of the text); in the apotheosis (or divinization) into which these auxiliaries gather the human subject; and, most importantly for me, in the ambiguity that attaches to Freud's use of the word 'organ'.

With the formulation of 'organ' there is an uncertainty as to whether Freud is addressing the technical tools with which the human has burdened herself or, more disconcertingly perhaps, whether he is proposing that our biological sense-organs are themselves little more than the remote fleshy equivalents of those troublesome devices and are equally estranged from some inner, more ancient psychic realm. Although the notion of our sense-organs as something distinguishable from ourselves is a precarious one in a world that has had to learn the lessons of phenomenology, I like this potential interpretation of the fragment of Freud's writing. It suggests that processes of sensorial engagement, like that of listening, can themselves be approached as if they were auxiliaries—requiring learning, amenable to adaptation, occasionally unwieldy.

It is intriguing that in the essays we have commissioned here, despite the diverse range of technical and conceptual devices on display, there is a recurring focus on the potential of the apparatus to alter the scale and pace of the spatio-temporal encounter.

For David Hendy radio becomes a site of expansion and contraction, its audience caught between rapt attention and distraction, encountering the register of high culture, succeeded by more vernacular voice, where listening alone is simultaneously a listening together. For Salomé Voegelin, radio has shifted from the big wooden box to something that is accessed through other peripherals, through computers and their miniaturised versions. Yet that same sense of the collapsing of distance persists, not the far-off flickering of television's "visual wars" but something closer, connected, something alone-together. Some of the other media that McLuhan spoke about get drawn into the undertow of these contributors' accounts: Jessica Cawley's research demonstrates that "although recordings can physically, visually or emotionally distance the listener and performer, the opposite is also true; recordings have the ability to link musical communities over vast distances and bring people close together;" Michael Chanan speaks of another 'community' that is established by a listening technology when he explores how "through the different spaces of the film" a cinema audience finds itself shifted between precise recognition of the identity of the music being mobilised and an familiarity with "musics we cannot name". LaBelle details the construction of an apparatus that yokes three performers together, readying them to accept contributions from the audience and enabling them to return those contributions 'transcribed' and 'translated'. Yet our listening devices can also conspire to warp spatial relations into bleaker textures; in the last paragraphs of his essay, Peter Szendy imagines the microphone and recorder having inaugurated a *panacoustic* society of auditory surveillance far beyond any dreamed up in the pages of literary experiment or in the skewed fantasies of utilitarian philosopher and would-be social architect Jeremy Bentham.

Listening devices are not only amenable to being thought through in terms of their capacity to connect 'communities' across spacetime. They can also be understood as probes that are sent out into the world, equipped with arrays of sensors and primed to stream information back to the sender. For *Flood Tide*, John Eacott plunges a specialist measuring system into an expanse of moving water and uses his custom-built software to decode tidal data into real-time musical notation, providing the river-side performers with a score that effectively allows the audience to listen to the tide. Davide Tidoni's approach narrows the panoply of technological encumbrances down to an inflatable balloon and a sharp pin, these props enabling an echo-locative exploration of architectural space and—as the transcript makes audible—of overlapping political territories. Dawn Scarfe's *Listening Glasses* provide a more solitary encounter, the delicate, resonant orbs being gently pushed into the opening of the ear, vibrating in sympathy with tones in the acoustic environment. Scarfe's *Glasses* are perhaps emblematic of this category of listening device—the device listens first so that we may listen after. Volkmar Klien provides a powerful corrective to those accounts which propose a delegation of the responsibility for listening to the devices themselves—as he carefully argues, the scientists' working definition of listening is by no means exhaustive. "But it would be naive for sonic artists to uncritically celebrate the new tools simply as means to further improve their bachelor machines. (And yet, were they unable to listen, could they ever truly obey?)."

Brandon LaBelle

....

Tender Beats

Reflections on a performance with Sina Khani & Pedro Inês
as part of DNK series, Amsterdam, 2008

*To engage the particulars of a given context, by way of the ear, remains
a continual project, informing my activities as an artist. Sound in this
way is not only material, but a means for staging performative events
that generate relational narratives and the making of shared space.
Exploring such strategies, I presented a performance in Amsterdam
in 2008 where the audience was invited to bring their favourite CDs,
including music, field recordings or archival material. These were played
to two performers, a singer and a writer, who listened to the different CDs
over headphones (the audience never heard what they heard). In response
to what they were listening to, the singer spoke, sang, whispered, and
made small performative gestures, while the writer described the sounds,
or the music, trying to convey to the audience the particular qualities.
This writing was projected using an overhead projector. In addition, as
a third performer, I sat at a table with a computer and focused on what
the other two were doing: I listened to the singer, his words and vocals,
and I read what the writer wrote, his descriptions, his feelings about the
sounds, his impressions. In response, I wrote another text, which was also
projected into the space, as a way to give narrative to the overall situation.
I would pick up lyrics from the singer, I would grab a single word from
the writer, and bring these together into a story. I became a storyteller,
trying to incorporate this live material into my own thinking, my own
memories, my own listening, and to give the audience a reflection of the
very music or sounds they had brought to the event. The performance
acted as a process of translation and transcription, extending the idea
of context through the making of an event in which multiple elements,
around practice and reflection, narrative and sound, might interact. The
experience for myself, as participant, was extremely enlivening: I found
that my listening was both an external register, of what was occurring,
in the scene, and an internal process of remembering, recalling into the
room past experiences of what I might call my first listening. In this sense,
I found myself caught in a network of auditory material and reference, as
a sort of impressionable body.*

Text from the performance written live:

My friend, Tommy, he always wanted to be a rock star. I guess, it was his dream. A kind of rhythm of the heart. This song inside. A sort to tap, tap, tapping... a recurring passion. He would spend hours at home, listening to Kraftwerk, Hawkwind, Gang of Four... singing. The neighbours, they would laugh. I took him serious. A kind emerging idea... something dark, darker, like a hum. Inside. Tap, tap, tapping. One day, I thought, yeah, a rock star. So, while Tommy sang, I went out and got a drum kit. Suddenly, there it was, my own... rhythm of the heart. A song, an endless chord, that started to resound, break, thump, a noise, something restless. I was caught. A sort of Click, that opened up a door...

The song, it came like an invisible vapour, a tune from some corner, like a melody... floating in, blowing in from nowhere, capturing my attention. It wouldn't stop... It was, we might say, an answer: no, a beginning. That melody, that rhythm, what was that? A bolt of energy, a rapture, a voice... No, a form of organisation: like, a structure to the raw fascination and desiring flux of the self. Crazy. That is what I needed. A new form. So, Tommy and I, we got together. To share that energy, that inside rhythm. A shared breath. A pulse. Crashing in. To take over, a force that began to fill the space, the days, something haunting, but, that is, concrete. A possibility. What I started to think, could be, Happiness. Love.

The rhythm inside, then, suddenly was outside. A sort of Beat, that broke, and then started some other gathering, Together. That is, between You and I. To let it come out, to recognise everything is possible, a horizon. No really, I'm not exaggerating. Everything started. The unfolding, the gathering, the break in the system, the force of an idea: the making of a new body. But nothing in words— that was it, nothing in words. Tommy singing, the hit of the drum, and then, the beginning of a melody. To follow it, was to come together, and to make a statement: to be a rock star. Tragedy and Comedy in one. Friends and strangers, in one space.

The instrument was only a sort of beginning, the rest was made in the moment of listening. Moving. Energy. A sort of fluid. Without shape, but totally determined, and full of consequence. Urgent. To make a difference. Contrast: you have that over there, but, then you have this over here. Noise. Like something trying to get in, scratching at the door, tapping under the floor, beating, no, hoping. It says, "can I come in?" I wait. For some other word, to follow: a gift—like the day when Tommy takes out a new record, something by Zoviet

France, and he says, "hey, check this out." New sound. Or, like the day when, after hours of recording, he turns the volume up, looks back at me, a little drunk, and lets out this incredible laugh—I thought, *Yes, that's it*. The laugh, this wild mysterious laugh, said so much: like a noise full of meaning, that is, arriving in this instant, of being more. Excess. Excitement.

But, maybe I'm getting carried away...

Maybe it is more basic: like in the morning, you wake, up, something cloudy, uncertain, a beginning. But, often, there is suddenly, there, in the head, a song—you know, that feeling. That moment, when suddenly, you find yourself singing some song, without even thinking. In the morning. Something maybe you haven't heard in years. It breaks in. Slips through. Like a breath, a vibration, from below, and then out—the words leave the mouth, a lyric, and you must, at least, laugh at yourself, a little. But also, enjoy the situation: the rhythm of the heart. Like a door opening. The inside, coming out. It fills the room: erupts, takes over, a vibration, and then, a voice. To become a theme. Something you carry along into the day: to refer back to, during lunch, or, at the café. It continues. A friend. Noise. Maybe it operates, like a shadow. It is there, you know, as shadows are, without real definition. But then, like shadows do, it gives definition: a sort of absence, making present, what is always already there.

I like the shadow. This, thing which is always no-thing. Like a breath. Or, maybe, like a sound. That fills, without being finished. A beginning and end, in one. An atmosphere. Maybe that's what I heard, that day, with Tommy laughing, a kind of: shadow. It took over, and then, was gone. I recognised, the meaning. An invitation. Where one could join in. Not that loneliness wouldn't persist, no, but that at least, there was someone else. Silence, of course, is always there. A stop. Like when, at the end of the day, taking off the shoes, you leave something behind. To enjoy what comes next. Silence, that is always already a noise. That's the beauty: Both, Together. The shadow, and the light. A rhythm. Tap, tap, tapping. Back, and forth. Memory.

Things unfold. But, things, also, echo. Back and forth. The beginning and the end, together. Music. Like a thread, going from there, to here. Or, like a balloon, which is, of course, a captured breath: held, inside, to carry forward, that energy, to, somewhere, else. I always thought, the balloon floating in the sky, was like a lost breath. A body, someone's. And if you were to find that balloon, open it up, slowly, you would receive, that breath. To let it, out slowly, against one's own lips. To inhale, that other breath, that had floated, from somewhere. Or, to hear it. Suddenly. A voice.

Davide Tidoni

....

A Balloon for the Barbican —Politics of Listening in The City of London

Characters
YOU, the researcher who investigates space by listening to its acoustic qualities.
POLICEMAN, his duty is to ensure community safety and maintain public order.
POLICEWOMAN, her role is to prevent crime and improve security.
MANAGER OF THE ESTATE, he is responsible for the happiness and comfort of the residents.

Scene
The Barbican, City of London, UK, January 2012.
All characters are fictitious; any reference to real facts or people is purely coincidental.

Act I
Friday afternoon. 3pm.

Scene 1
The balloon is fully inflated. You are waiting for the right moment to pop it to listen to the echo bouncing off the surrounding buildings. You stand still with open ears. Suddenly two cops approach you from one of the public courtyards of the Barbican Estate.

POLICEMAN You al'right?
YOU Hi.
POLICEMAN What are you up to?
YOU What? Sorry?
POLICEWOMAN What are you up to?
YOU Ahhh… I'm doing a research project, it's basically about the acoustics of the place and I'm popping balloons here in the courtyard.

POLICEMAN Do you have a permit?

POLICEWOMAN Do you have a permit?

YOU Yes.

POLICEMAN Have you got it with you?

YOU No, it's not printed.

POLICEMAN Right OK, because obviously we have seen you walking along... *(interrupted)*

POLICEWOMAN We don't mind you doing stuff but our office is there and we saw you walking on that ledge.

POLICEMAN Yeah, eh... *(interrupted)*

POLICEWOMAN How many people live here?

POLICEMAN Yeah, you... *(interrupted)*

YOU How many people!? *(thinking about the connections between population density, surveillance and accepted behaviours in public spaces)*

POLICEWOMAN Yeah, lot of people, if they see you they might call us in, so we need to be aware of this... err...

YOU Ah!

POLICEMAN You are walking around popping balloons and you might be disturbing residents here, while obviously some of them, I mean not all of them would be out at work, lots of elderly residents here will be asleep and everything... and you are just bursting balloons and obviously the way like... you know yourselves, you are doing a thing on it, like the Barbican, all the sound echoes around, so... I mean we heard the balloon all the way down there bursting and everything like that.

POLICEWOMAN It echoes a lot, you know that, acoustics wise, it echoes a lot, stuff like that.

POLICEMAN So... I don't know, if you want to go and do it outside the Barbican that's fine.

YOU Well, the point of my research is to do it here inside the Barbican and... *(interrupted)*

POLICEMAN Do you have any ID on you or anything like that? What I'll do is if I can take your name and everything like that. If we receive... err... no one has complained to us yet but if anybody complains you will have to stop straight away and that'll be the end of it.

YOU Sure, OK, but can I pop this last balloon because I've already blown it up and then I'll give you my ID.

POLICEMAN Fair enough, I suppose. *(resigned, as if something undesirable cannot be avoided)*

Baaang!!! The sound of the balloon echoes around bouncing back and forth off the building's concrete walls.

POLICEMAN You see that's quite loud, you are disturbing people as they are walking through and that's why you have to stop.

POLICEWOMAN That's your last one, yeah?

POLICEMAN Yes, so that's the last one, yes?

YOU No.

POLICEMAN Yes!

YOU We can do this together if you want.

POLICEMAN No we can't do it together, basically you are gonna have to stop because if we get complaints... Yeah, like I said!

YOU No already? No, it's not possible, already?

POLICEMAN The people are living, look, how far are you from that window?

YOU Yes, but c'mon it was just one second!

POLICEMAN No, no, no, mate, you might be waking people up... *(interrupted)*

POLICEWOMAN We're telling you now, we let you do that one, yeah, we let you do that, all right?

YOU The last one?

POLICEMAN No, you have done the last one!

POLICEWOMAN We let you just do that one, you listen to us now: no more that's it, that's it!

POLICEMAN No more yeah, you are gonna have to stop now.

YOU Why do they... *(interrupted while trying to explain the constructive value of noise as opportunity for social interaction and unexpected encounters)*

POLICEWOMAN This is a private area! You understand there are people living here!

POLICEMAN *(attempting to pacify the situation)* I'll tell you what, if you come down with me to the Barbican Estate Office, we are gonna speak to the Estate Office. If they are happy for you to do it, that's fine, if they say no, then no.

POLICEWOMAN Come with us we'll go speak to them now.

YOU OK.

The two police officers leave the public courtyard and lead You to the Estate Office.

Scene 2

MANAGER OF THE ESTATE Hi, how are you doing?

POLICEWOMAN *(patronisingly)* We saw this gentleman recording outside our police office, this guy *(pointing)* walking on the ledge which is 20 foot up, don't know if he has got a permit for that, and he's bursting balloons as well.

POLICEMAN He says he's doing an acoustic test; he said he's got permission to do it. What we are just worried about is… if you are happy for him to do it, it's fine but I've seen people, next to, err… outside people's houses and obviously if we get complaints…

MANAGER Yes, it's a residential area.

POLICEWOMAN He's got big balloons and he set them off outside the residents' flats. Popping them, it's really loud.

POLICEMAN Yea, so, what we don't want is complaints coming in but if you lot are happy for him to do it…

MANAGER Were you walking along the ledge of the wall?

POLICEMAN Yes.

YOU No.

POLICEMAN He was.

POLICEWOMAN Yep.

YOU Well the project is not about that, I was walking there because I found it interesting to walk there but… *(interrupted)*

MANAGER Well, of course in general I would prefer if you didn't walk along the parapet wall, quite frankly.

YOU Yes but I'm from the countryside and I climb trees every day.

MANAGER Yea, but we don't climb concrete in the city.

POLICEMAN If you fall off over here…

POLICEWOMAN People would ring and say someone is trying to commit something and so on.

MANAGER And also, the most important thing is, I've got to clear you up, when you are splattered on the public high walk afterwards and quite frankly I'm not happy about that.

POLICEWOMAN Yeah, and we would have to get lots of bodies to cordon off the area.

YOU So there's no way we can continue today, right?

MANAGER No, this is where people live, you know, it's unfair, if I came and banged big balloons outside your flat…

YOU We were thinking to do this again from 10 to 11 this evening.

MANAGER No. No, no, definitely no, no, I would say no, the noisy… err… time you can make a noise here is between 10 in the morning and 4 in the afternoon; because again, I will quote, it's a residential area.

YOU The thing is that at that time the background noise is very loud and you cannot hear the sound reflections from the buildings.

POLICEMAN But at 10 o'clock and 11 o'clock when you want to do it people are gonna be sleeping...

POLICEWOMAN People are going to be sleeping ready to go to work the next day and so on.

POLICEMAN ...and you are gonna be waking them up with balloons and they are not gonna be happy.

POLICEWOMAN They are gonna call us and we won't be happy.

POLICEMAN We won't be happy.

YOU OK, so the best time you say is between 10am and 4pm.

MANAGER Well, it is not the best time, is the only time that you are allowed to do that kind of thing.

To be continued...

The project *A Balloon for the Barbican* was first presented at *Bang! Being the Building. A Musarc Salon at the Barbican* on the 26th of January 2012 as part of the OMA/Progress exhibition at the Barbican Gallery, City of London, UK.

John Eacott

Listening to Tide: Ideas and Practice Behind 'Flood Tide'

Flood Tide is a sonification of tidal flow in which the speed of moving water is mapped to musical notation and performed by a group of musicians. The effect is a musical composition rendered by tide. This practice has evolved naturally from my interests in music, software programming and a love of the sea, sailing and navigation.

The work has been performed ten times. Starting in 2008 with a quartet of marimba, vibraphone and two celli, it increased the following year to sextet with the addition of bass clarinet and alto flute. For the Thames Festival in  September 2009, 31 professional and volunteer musicians took part including orchestral instruments, voices and Japanese taiko drums. The largest performance in July 2010 at London's Southbank involved 39 musicians performing a full 6 hour incoming tide.

So why is a translation of tide flow data into music interesting to audiences? Is it so that we can hear something that is normally very quiet or silent? Mindful of the impositions placed on our already rich aural lives, making sound from an event that is normally silent may seem unnecessary and even unwelcome.

Often, musicians rely on ideas and inspiration to compose music. *Flood Tide*, on the other hand, is a process from which musical material emerges. As a musician and composer myself, there is a part of me that welcomes lifting the burden to generate ideas and to be creative. Because it is now possible to generate musical ideas instantaneously as a result of the kinds of process employed in *Flood Tide*, it seems attractive to harness them, to remove human creativity on the level of choosing notes, harmonies and rhythms from the equation and let the process unfold.

Of course human creativity is still involved. Not at the level of choosing notes but in the design of algorithms, the processes that select the notes and make the music. Creating an algorithm is both simple and challenging. The simple part happens in the form of an idea such as—wouldn't it be good if the music did… something or other… in relation to the tide? For instance, in *Flood Tide* the tempo of the music—how rapidly beats of the music pass—is a simple conversion of the tide rate. So when the water moves slowly the music is slow and when the water moves quickly so does the music. There are algorithms for generating rhythm, choosing the pitches, choosing a playing instruction (arco, pizzicatto, tremolo etc.) and for vocalists the choice of text, and finally an algorithm that decides which instruments are playing. This is designed to represent the tide rate in an obvious way, too—when tide is slow there are few musicians, when it is faster there are more.

A more challenging part of writing an algorithm is converting the idea to working computer code. As a non-trained computer programmer, this is always demanding but also deeply absorbing. Before writing my first line of computer code in 1984, I remember wanting to avoid working with computers as I believed it would be mechanical and soulless. On the contrary, programming computers, particularly to take part in creative acts, is absorbing, deeply creative and very human.

I strive to make each algorithm simple and clear in itself. One feature I have observed, both in my own work and in the computer music of others, is that it is easy to generate complexity. It is as easy for a computer process to generate a million bars of a million notes as it is to generate a few bars with few notes. While complexity is easy, it is more challenging to strive for clarity, meaning and structures that audiences can understand.

The result does not have to be bland, however. Although the algorithms themselves are simple, a complex interaction occurs between them. The rhythm algorithm effectively chooses which of the notes selected by the pitch algorithm are included in a musical phrase. This phrase is subject to a playing instruction, choice of musicians and tempo. The result is a kind of emergent behaviour, a rich or complex output arising from simple rules.

It is accepted that digital technologies have made the production, distribution and consumption of music easier. While this ease is welcome, it has also made things that were previously unachievable possible. Whereas musical composition has conventionally occurred in advance, followed by a realisation of the work with musicians, digital technologies permit the compression of this timeline into an instant. When Felix Mendelssohn visited Britain in 1829 and composed *Fingal's Cave*, inspired by a trip to the Hebrides, he used the latest composition tools and ideas available to him to represent that location with music. With *Flood Tide* I also use contemporary ideas and tools to make a composition generated by the actual condition of a place at that moment.

This task of writing algorithms for this kind of sonification involves balancing contradictory demands. Firstly, there is a need to represent the data clearly so that it is apparent, if not obvious, to the listener what the tide is doing—whether the tide is slow, fast, increasing or decreasing. Listeners that take in more than a few minutes of the performance should learn something of the overall shape that tide makes. The second consideration is to make music. To some extent the need to construct interesting music conflicts with the need to represent data and I will offer a brief statement about some of the musical or aesthetic considerations assumed here. There are a vast or unlimited range of approaches and values one may take in generating music and my own preferences and cultural factors play a part.

It would make practical sense perhaps to realise the music electronically. It is completely feasible, if not considerably easier, to create a mapping of the tidal data which affects the output of oscillators and synthesisers. Instead live musicians playing acoustic instruments are used. This is partly a personal preference for live instruments, with the spectacle of seeing them played and the richness, imperfections and dramas that live performance involves. While orchestral instruments, strings, wind, brass and tuned percussion form the core of the group, the use of voices has evolved as a versatile component, and Japanese Taiko drums inject a strongly rhythmic element and add power to the faster and more energetic parts. Practical considerations also affect the choice of instruments: can they be played outdoors without electricity? Can the instrument be played for a long time? For *Flood Tide*, the first and only time we have sonified a full incoming tide lasting just under 6 hours, jazz soloists were involved to offer further variation of content and style. The jazz soloists were asked to improvise in response to a scale and rhythm generated algorithmically to allow them to use the orchestra as a luxurious accompaniment to their solo.

Tide is not normally listened too. It can be heard if you have the inclination to get close to tidal water that is moving quickly. As tidal water passes fixed objects like rocks, piers, walls or moored boats, the turbulence generated which creates waves, eddies and sometimes broken water dissipates its energy as pressure, a slight temperature increase and sound. Often this sound is unnoticed as it mixes with the sound of other waves, wind, birds etc.

Tide has a particular and—for the most part—predictable structure. If you open a nautical almanac you will see a graph used to predict the height of tide and this is related to the mathematical sinusoid. A graph of predicted rate of flow is also sinusoidal (albeit with a different phase, like the relationship between graphs of sine and cosine). Actual rate of flow is somewhat different, however. The graph below represents two and a half hours of tide. Along with a generally sinusoidal trajectory are many other twists and turns. I have speculated with oceanographers about the causes of this variation and reached no definitive conclusion. Disturbances caused by river traffic is one possibility, although I prefer to think that we are seeing harmonics and resonances of the main tidal wave as it reflects off the river banks and any other physical objects in the river. In this way a tide wave behaves just like a sound wave affected by the acoustic properties of a particular room.

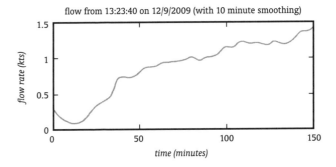

flow from 13:23:40 on 12/9/2009 (with 10 minute smoothing)

Flood Tide is a long term project. Before the first performance in 2008 the idea had been gestating for 5 or 6 years. Performances normally take around a year to organise, getting funding, finding musicians, making changes to the software and dealing with practical and planning issues. There have been suggestions to make a performance of *Flood Tide* with a professional symphony orchestra, and invitations from around the UK and beyond to create sonification performances, making the best of local musicians at their particular stretch of tidal water.

David Hendy

The Undercoat of Life —Listening to Radio

People write to broadcasters a lot. To television celebrities especially, of course. But to radio people too. Indeed once, when I was immersed in the BBC's archives, one of the things I discovered was just how *many* people have been writing in about the radio they'd heard— radio they'd loved, hated, been stimulated by, *disturbed* by. The numbers are mind-boggling. I took a year at random and counted the correspondence. In 1970, the BBC received 227,167 letters or phone-calls about its programmes. This figure doesn't include the much larger number of fan-letters addressed directly to programme-presenters, just those written to the Corporation centrally. And of these, 128,626—well *over* half—were about radio. As it happened, the overwhelming majority of these were about Radio 4. At the time, it was this that interested me most. It seemed to confirm, not just that the Radio 4 audience was a letter-writing one par excellence, but that the lingering popularity of speech radio was the result of some deep affinity to hearing the human voice through our radio sets. There was something about the desire for human connection, the warm intimacy of a friendly voice, the understandable need to avoid feeling horribly alone in an otherwise empty house. And when you read the letters themselves, you can sense this. "A rich source of pleasure"... "An old friend, comfortable, amusing, helpful and informative"... "I had my sanity saved by it". And so on.

Yet all this devotion is not just about radio listening as cosy, domestic companionship. It's more epic than that. The American media historian Susan Douglas describes the distinctive pleasures of listening to radio at night, sitting in the darkened car or lying in bed: "tuned to a disembodied voice or music", she writes, "evokes a spiritual, almost telepathic contact across space and time, a reassurance that we aren't alone in the void". Certainly night's shadows provide an edge to our aural experience: the greater the absence of visual distraction, poets and psychologists tell us, the larger the space for contemplation and imagination. There's definitely a cognitive basis, then, for that time-worn phrase that "the pictures are better on radio", and it would appear that the innate pleasure we find in stimulating our imagination in this way helps forge a strong *emotional* attachment to the radio medium itself. But something still more profound goes on when we listen to the radio. It's something tied-up with both its *liveness* and its nature as something *broadcast*. Radio offers a myriad of sounds scattered widely through the ether for all to catch, but which then melt in front of our ears.

Being live and being broadcast, listening to the radio generates a powerful sense of participation, a collective sensibility even. As we listen alone at home, we're also aware that others elsewhere are listening to the same thing at the same time; we unify around a common experience. Radio, in other words, prompts us to explore our innermost thoughts, but it also takes us out of ourselves. It allows for idiosyncratic mental images *and* for the shared experience. Sudden mental contact is made—a brief flash of recognition or understanding. And here the simultaneous and ephemeral nature of it all is crucial. What's heard is somehow real, the voices and sounds of people alive—though invisible—at that moment of hearing. Our contact with them is emotional, as well as intellectual. And if we miss this moment? Well, too bad. Because radio, though a pervasive background to our lives, and increasingly available to 'listen again' online or via podcasts, still speaks the language of liveness. So it still offers a kind of *eventfulness*.

The 'we-feeling' of radio is vague, shifting, multiple, of course. Like our identities, it's sometimes national, sometimes local, sometimes cultural or ethnic or political. Collective sensibility is a protean thing. Radio stations worry about this. Since they usually have a 'target' audience in mind, they like identities to be stable. But, thankfully, there's rarely a perfect junction between sender and receiver. Broadcasting is a scattering in all directions: anyone within reach might tune-in. Or not. And this risk, this sheer wastefulness is... delicious. *They*, the broadcasters, never really know who's listening, or with how much attentiveness. *We*, the audience, can choose to listen, or not—choose to listen *attentively*, or not. Radio's sounds are in the ether, waiting to be reeled in—or, just as often, left wandering unheard. When we let them into our homes it isn't because they've forced their way in. They don't *demand* consumption—or indeed any response at all.

Interactivity is today's God. But the passivity radio listening allows should not be seen as failure. The power's all in our own hands. We're receiving a gift, really. We might well be moved or appalled or upset by what we hear on the radio; sometimes we might be indifferent. But whatever we feel consciously, we're almost always being 'interactive' inside our heads when listening, even if we think its outpourings drift by with barely a flicker of attention. Radio arrives so *easily*, then sneaks right under the radar. And the effects of this kind of listening are cumulative. The painter Tom Phillips once described radio as an 'undercoat' of sound that supported his art. It's been unobtrusively in the background of his life, he said—always has been, always would be. Because of this, it would "employ and free" his mind. Behind every shape and stripe of colour on the canvas, he said, lay "traces of my radio days—a lifetime's cricket, a thousand plays". For him, radio was a "sightless Odeon" where voices "aloof but warm" materialised imperceptibly. They did not force him to attend to them so much as quietly ingratiated themselves into his mind.

What mattered for Tom Phillips—what matters for most of us—is not just radio's presence. It's also radio's content. For at its best, radio is promiscuous—putting in front of our ears a cluttered mosaic of fact and fiction, high culture and low, the demotic and the high-flown, the banal and the significant. As in the world of literature, it provides a continuously unfolding field of comparisons and contrasts, spreading infinitely outwards—it provides, in other words, the raw materials of thought. Here, perhaps, radio even surpasses litera-ture. For it is not just generous to those who can't read; it is more pervasive than books; it also goes on-and-on. This jumbled aural tapestry—sounds, music, voices rubbing up against one another—generates, in almost Proustian fashion, a host of associations and memories. We often decry radio for its failure to accommodate acous-tic experiment, its *artlessness*. Where, we cry, is radio's avant-garde? But really that's beside the point. For when we listen to the radio we *need* it to be self-effacing, to be a kind of empty vessel. What we hear—what most of us *want* to hear—is a corridor through which the rest of the whole noisy, argumentative, fascinating, and sometimes, yes, *beautiful* world passes before us. A corridor available at the flick of a switch. In the 21st century, that's still rather magical, isn't it?

Salomé Voegelin

A Short History of Radio Listening

I do not listen to the radio, I listen to the computer playing the radio, I listen to the iPod replaying the radio, I watch on YouTube videos of people in radio studios making radio, I listen on DAB. The air is thin here, no more waves, no more voices of the dead hiding in the murmur of the lost signal. The uncertain fuzz of analogue radio is gone and with it its poetry, flattened into a perfect signal: clear, faultless but thin. I am sure there is poetry in that thin flatness of the digital, something new, a different metaphor that people will bemoan when *it* is gone, I am just not sure what *it* is yet.

My granddad listened to the radio, a big great wooden thing, big as a cupboard, made from shiny wood with ivory tuning dials.

He sat in front of it most afternoons and evenings, perched on a heavy wooden armchair upholstered with a flower-patterned fabric, leaning slightly forward so as to glean every word that came through the ether.

My grandma would bring him coffee and biscuits and she embroidered little rectangular coverlets to put on the armrests of the chair to protect them from the grease of his chafing suit jacket and the coffee stains.

I overhear it as I do the dishes, iron, tidy up or work. It's there, I am there, no leaning forward required. I am not that interested in what it says, I only need it to sound.

My grandma hated it, she much rather wanted to go to dances, meet friends, be out and about, but the voices from the wooden box held my granddad indoors, ears glued. She heard it, he needed to listen. He needed to know what was being said out there about the great stories of the day.

I have to sit in front of the computer constantly linked to web-sites, emails, Facebook. No dancing for me either, other things going on that I just simply need to be part of and check in to.

My granddad was part of one radio community. His was a shared listening, not with my gran, but with all the other people living within reach of its signal, who would all hear the same. This community was imagined but real. They all together alone followed the stories and news on the radio that put into words the reality of the world out there and furnished their worldview.

I am part of different communities on-line, many different ones to serve different aspects of the complex post-post-modern personality. These communities are not really out there, however, but are in here, in my machine with me, feeding a more solipsistic sense of reality.

My grandfather was a customs officer in the Second World War. The voices speaking on the wireless were vital for him to understand the situation, his own purpose and position: Who to let in, who to keep out.

I am inseparably joined to the internet, which insidiously merges my leisure and work and produces them as one boundariless activity: a shapeless whole, with little purpose and not much scope to differentiate.

My grandmother let the refugees in through the back door of the customs officer's house, whose garden bordered on enemy land, and out through the front into her own country.

My granddad berated her, believing she just did not understand the severity of the situation. She should have listened to the radio to understand what was at stake.

My grandma thought it was lives at stake: people, families, the real world we live in.

My parents did not care much for the radio, and still don't. The last one broke years ago and sits still unrepaired in their basement. They read, and then they bought a telly, a little white plastic one that showed black and white images. They lived Vietnam, the Cold War and the conflict in Bosnia and Herzegovina on that little box. Theirs were visual wars, remote and without consequences, not the call to arms my granddad had experienced.

My parents' little black and white telly broke down when my mum did an all night Formula One session, it went straight up in flames. Now they have a flat screen one but they still watch only the analogue channels: German detective stories mainly.

I listen to the rebels in Libya, Egypt, Bahrain... all on-line. Flicking between newspaper, Al Jazeera TV, BBC radio, Twitter messages and YouTube appeals, I live vicariously through their lives a revolution that I will not have. They are not out there, they are in here together with all the other communities I gathered up on my machine and that fill my life with information, opinions, a sense of self and things to do that I will never do because of the life in here that needs to be seen to and written about.

My parents both worked in industries that did not rely on news from the front. Cosied up in the post-war boom the connection had become irrelevant. It was about something else, about entertainment and things happening somewhere over there. They did not listen together and neither made coffee or biscuits for the other. Instead they sat and stared into one box.

My grandfather's listening was ideological and political. He heard a rallying call and took it as a cue how to live his life, what side to take, what wars to fight.

My listening is tautological. I listen to listen. Maybe I mutter to myself in-between or write something on Facebook or rant in an email, and then I go back to listening without hearing much.

My grandparents' phone hung on the corridor wall, incoming calls only.

My parents' phone sits on a little table next to the settee, on its very own carpet. It is a short message machine to say hello, to ask how you are and to arrange for you to come over. My mum does not really know how to hold a longer conversation on the phone, she cannot listen unseen and so she only talks, breathless and fast and then hangs up.

My sister Skypes for hours.

My phone does everything. It connects me to my various communities that are always with me in miniature form on the little screen of my BlackBerry. I am never alone. No need to be restless pushing the children on the swings, no need to feel awkward waiting for somebody. There are things to listen to, podcasts to download, emails to check, Facebook friends to poke...

The radio has shrunk from the big hefty cupboard thing of my granddad to the little black shiny thing in my pocket. It allows me to listen on the go but also stops me from doing anything about the heard as I am constantly listening on the go.

My granddad retired and went travelling, everywhere, all over the world: Nepal, Mexico, the Amazon, India, Afghanistan.

I connect daily to lots of global on-line communities, communicate with people all over the world.

Michael Chanan

Listening to Music in the Cinema

Listening to music in the cinema is not quite the transparent or innocent experience it might seem, partly because music itself is neither transparent nor innocent, and partly because of the peculiarities of the film medium.

Music's relation to cinema is, in Jacques Derrida's terms, that of the supplement—an added element which is nonetheless integral to the whole, like the preface to a book, or the newspaper which is not complete without its supplement. We readily think of it this way: first, because cinema began as moving pictures with no sound (though increasingly presented with live musical accompaniment), and second, because of the manner of its incorporation into the soundtrack when the sound film arrived and rapidly acquired the epithet 'the talkies'—because speech is primary. To be sure, sound cinema was also about musicals, but otherwise, except when a story called for musical performance in front of the camera, the music was added in afterwards—the very model of the paradoxical status of Derrida's supplement, being outside the narrative ('extra-diegetic') but still part of the film.

Music in the cinema, like everything else you hear, is acousmatic —it comes through loudspeakers, a form of mechanical reproduction which our culture has fully naturalised. In the cinema it is also subject to synchresis, a term used by Michel Chion for the capture of sound by the picture when picture and sound coincide and make contact: the mental fusion of sound and vision, transparent in the case of speech but often with illusory and paradoxical results. (Think Jacques Tati.) No sound is ever quite fixed, but, on the contrary, easily moves back and forth, speech included, between the different spaces of the film—on-screen; just off-screen; and extra-diegetic, outside the space of the narrative, invisible. Music, however, is particularly slippery. When accompanying music coincides with action on the screen it's called 'mickey- mousing'—like the cartoon. But when it isn't subsumed into the visual, and doesn't actively push itself forward, it simply recedes into the background. Unless it comes forward to envelop the picture, like Prokofiev's music for *Alexander Nevsky*.

The acousmatic background, however, is a funny space, invisible, virtual, extremely plastic—elastic, ductile, pliable—and full of voices, sound, noise and music of every variety. Unlike the acoustic background of everyday life, which advances and recedes and moves around with you, the acousmatic background cannot be entered or even approached because it isn't physical. But it never quite 'disappears'. When it flattens out, it collapses into an insistent heard silence.

The conventional wisdom of the film industry—that background music isn't there to be listened to but merely heard—is a terrible simplification, because it all depends: firstly on what type of listener you are, secondly what type of music it is, and thirdly the mode of listening (attentive or distracted etc.).

Sometimes accompanying music is intended to call attention to itself—think of the menacing motif of danger in *Jaws* (composer: John Williams). Sometimes it calls attention to itself without intending to, because even if only half-heard, it resonates with the potpourri of musical traces we carry around in our heads. For example, a musically knowledgeable listener will likely pick up in Michael Nyman's score for *The End of the Affair* an echo of a song from Leonard Bernstein's *West Side Story*, which in turn echoes a phrase from the slow movement of Beethoven's *Emperor* Concerto. The result is a chain of associations (or 'intertexts') which define the reach of the listener's musical world. The link from Nyman to Bernstein falls within the ken of anyone familiar with popular musical theatre, although many film-goers will spot the phrase without being able to name it, simply because Bernstein's song is so frequently heard on radio and television that it forms part of the musical background of the mainstream media, whose fragments embed themselves in collective musical memory (especially when advertising recycles them and turns them into fetish objects).

This collective musical memory is also a product of cinema from its earliest days, in parallel with records and radio, then television and lately an ever-expanding family of soundcarriers that nowadays include the internet cloud. Go back to the musical cue sheets which music publishers produced for silent movie pianists, in which they freely borrowed from the widest repertoire, including a great deal of classical art music. Everything was classified under easy access tabs so the pianist could flip to a new page quickly. In one edition from Schirmer's in 1924, Beethoven's 'Coriolan Overture' pops up under

Sinister. Under *Religioso* we find Handel's 'Largo', 'The Old Hundredth' by Bourgeois, 'Onward Christian Soldiers' by Sullivan, and the hymn 'Lead Kindly Light'. Under *Sadness* there are fourteen pieces by composers such as Beethoven, Chopin, Grieg, Anton Rubinstein, Tchaikovsky and Massenet, to mention only the best-known. Naturally pianists would often add in popular pieces of the day.

Film music has always been highly formulaic, often bordering on plagiarism. But also the opposite: driven to explore and invent new sounds, and the techniques for producing them—which then quickly join its ever expanding repertoire. Some of the most memorable film scores were written by composers who understood that cinema has its own sound palette and the sound space of music in the cinema is *sui generis*, and composed accordingly. In the 1930s, when acoustic quality was still limited, Joseph Kosma's guitarist humming to his own accompaniment in *Une partie de campagne*. In the 50s, the electronic score by Louis and Bebe Barron for *Forbidden Planet*. Or Ravi Shankar's score for the *Apu* trilogy.

The cue sheet system institutionalised what had already become established informal practice, in which a repertoire of well-known music was coded by loose and impressionistic iconic association. Here I follow Umberto Eco, who spoke of different types of musical sign, like military trumpet signals which have a specific denotation, or musical types (syntagms) like chorales, marches, waltzes, lullabies, etc., which derive their sign-value from social and cultural connotation (religious, military, social gatherings, domestic, etc.). A film like *Casablanca* (composer: Max Steiner) is full of them, on- and off-screen, including the climactic battle of song, when the crowd at Rick's Café join in the 'Marseillaise' to defeat the Nazis' German drinking song.

This kind of iconic association has become, through cinema, a major influence on the way we hear music, not just in the cinema but outside it too. T. W. Adorno spoke of what he called the "sensuous listener", in whom music stimulates visual images and vague reveries—like the poet Heine who wrote that Berlioz's music reminded him "of extinct species of animals, fabulous kingdoms, sky-storming impossibilities" and what-have-you. Cinema has a tendency to reinforce this tendency, not just for the casual listener but all of us at least some of the time.

There are also precious moments in cinema which depend not on affirming the conventional codes but in breaking them open in some way. Think of Kubrick's space-ship waltzing through the heavens to the swish of a Viennese waltz by Johann Strauss.

The long and the short of it is that the cinema audience comes to hear a very wide range of music without knowing what it is or who wrote it—perhaps until they find it on an album in a record store or hear it announced on the radio. This means that for the ordinary cinema-goer, the reach of the musical world is all-inclusive, but comprises a mélange of unnamed fragments of musics of greatly varying provenance. We all have wide familiarity with musics we cannot name and very likely wouldn't be interested in listening to otherwise, but when we hear them in their cinematic context, their cultural resonance does not wholly escape us. In short, music in the cinema, if we listen to it, presents us with a sense of a cultural world which is universal but diverse and polyphonic (and from which nothing in principle is excluded: here even noise can become musical). But whether you listen to it all depends...

Selected references

Adorno, T. W. 1972. *Introduction to the Sociology of Music*. New York: Seabury Press.
Chion, Michael. 1994. *Audio-vision, Sound on Screen*. New York: Columbia University Press.
Derrida, Jacques. 1976. '...That Dangerous Supplement...' in *Of Grammatology*. Baltimore: Johns Hopkins University Press.
Eco, Umberto. 1977. *A Theory of Semiotics*. London: Macmillan.

Volkmar Klien

The Artist and the Listening Machine

In recent decades, substantial work focusing on listening technologies emerged from several very active fields of research. As ready-to-use tools stemming from this basic research are slowly becoming available to sonic artists, it is important for artists and researchers alike to continuously reflect on the conceptualisations of human listening underlying these 'machine listening' approaches and their potential implications in sonic arts practice.

In the scientific community, there doesn't exist a single and uniform area of research referred to as 'machine listening', attempting to replicate human listening as such. The reasons for this are not primarily to be found in the lack of adequate technological solutions or machines fast enough to tackle the task. It simply cannot be taken as understood what human listening is, how it works, and how clearly it can be distinguished, not only from other modes of human perception and cognition, but also in terms of the individual listeners in their physical environment and cultural contexts. There is no single routine (or finite set of routines for that matter) of aural perception that could be automated by being modelled in code in order to replicate its functionality.

Scientists specialising in listening technology-related research come from a multitude of backgrounds ranging from psychology, acoustics, musicology and machine learning. They work on providing technological solutions to specific problems related to the realm of human listening, such as the recognition of spoken words, specific songs or sounds.[1] Even though any attempt to pull into dedicated paragraphs what are sizeable and active fields of research promises to over-simplify what is mentioned, while omitting numerous other areas of significance, the following will outline three fields, namely speech recognition, music information retrieval (MIR) and computational auditory scene analysis (CASA).[2]

---

1. For listening technologies it is normally of no importance if the solutions provided are in any way similar to what a human does when listening. They are judged by their success, not by their similarity to the human auditory system.

Speech recognition is the listening technology with the longest pedigree. It concerns itself with the transcription of spoken word into text and has come a long way since the presentation of the first tool for the recognition of spoken digits in 1952.[3] Today commercial packages for 'voice recognition' are readily available and speech recognition is in widespread use in—amongst others—areas of business, telephony and surveillance applications. Yet it is important to remember that converting spoken word to text is not a good analogue for what we normally mean by listening to somebody speak, where we would usually expect a certain understanding of what is actually being said—something that is not in itself part of speech recognition.

MIR is the interdisciplinary science of retrieving information from music in its various representations, such as scores or sound files. MIR researches and provides technologies for searching musical objects, or parts thereof, via queries framed in musical terms. One example of this would be a search through a database of songs by humming the hook-line of the specific song looked for. MIR evolves against the backdrop of the information society's needs for tools to manage its databases of sound and music, the size of which simply renders unaided 'manual' search unfeasible. Many 'real world' applications have stemmed from MIR's research and are in widespread use, for example in online music recommendation systems,[4] in signal-based play list generation systems[5] and music recognition systems.[6] To be able to successfully deliver the answers to user queries MIR does not restrict itself to the processing of data traditionally regarded as 'musical', such as scores and recordings, but instead includes data on how music is used by listeners. It does this by factoring in meta-data, such as that harvested from user tagging or tracking of user behaviour.

CASA is the study of auditory scene analysis by computational means.[7] In essence, CASA systems are 'machine listening' systems that aim to separate mixtures of sound sources in the same way

2. A more encompassing overview, accessible also to non-experts, is to be found in Polotti, Pietro and Rocchesso, Davide (eds.). 2008. *Sound to Sense, Sense to Sound. A State of the Art in Sound and Music Computing*. Berlin: Logos Verlag.

3. Davies, K.H., Biddulph, R. and Balashek, S. 1952. 'Automatic Speech Recognition of Spoken Digits', *Journal of the Acoustical Society of America*. 24(6) pp.637–642. Such as LastFM.

5. MOTS is a signal based playlist generation algorithm developed through a collaboration between Bang & Olufsen and OFAI, the Austrian Research Institute for Artificial Intelligence.

6. Such as Shazam.

7. Wang, DeLang and Brown, Guy J. (eds.). 2006. *Computational Auditory Scene Analysis: Principles, Algorithms and Applications*. Wiley-IEEE Press

that human listeners do. In his seminal book *Auditory Scene Analysis*,[8] Bregman describes the complexity of its task in the following metaphor: "Imagine that you are on the edge of a lake and a friend challenges you to play a game. The game is: Your friend digs two narrow channels up from the side of the lake. Each is a few feet long and a few inches wide and they are spaced a few feet apart. Halfway up each one, your friend stretches a handkerchief and fastens it to the sides of the channel. As waves reach the side of the lake they travel up the channels and cause the two handkerchiefs to go into motion. You are allowed to look only at the handkerchiefs and from their motions to answer a series of questions: How many boats are on the lake and what are they? Which is the most powerful one? Which one is closer? Is the wind blowing? Has any large object been dropped suddenly in the lake?" Regardless of the problematic underlying concept whereby human perception is interpreted as the building of internal representations of the outside world with the help of sense-data accessible via strictly separated modes of perception, Bregman's scenario (the lake representing the air surrounding us, the handkerchiefs our ear drums) successfully manages to depict the magnitude of the problems in digital signal processing associated with machine listening.

For sonic artists' listening technologies in their various guises can provide useful tools. While many of the technologies becoming available today are still in experimental phases, it has become clear already that the ability to produce different levels of content-awareness in machines will have distinct repercussions not only in the field of the production of sound and music, but also in redefining the roles these play in everyday life.

By applying these technologies as well as extending their use far beyond their standard application in market-driven software solutions, sonic artists can open up new horizons in the production as well as conceptualisation of their work. Sonic installations for example can now be designed to be (to a certain extent) aware of the soundscape they evolve in, enabling them to respond and adapt in real-time. New digital musical instruments may be created, allowing users to re-define their individual instrument by simply 'feeding' it soundfiles containing examples of the sonic qualities required. The list of possible applications is seemingly endless, stretching from instruments reacting automatically to other players, to semi- or

8. Bregman, Albert S. 1990. *Auditory Scene Analysis, The Perceptual Organization of Sound.* Cambridge, MA: MIT Press p.5

fully-automatic improvisers and generative music engines capable of mining databases of millions of songs for 'new inspiration'.

On the recipients' side these future technologies will strongly influence listening habits and modes of reception. Tools allowing the user to re-create and re-mix sound recordings or their own live sounding environment, on a perceptually informed level (for example, 'a car driving by') rather than on a purely technical level (for example, 'filtering the ~5000 hz band'), will help blur the lines between the traditional roles of producer[9] and recipient, shifting the focus further from static works of art to process-based approaches such as the dynamic re-shaping of real-world soundscapes, extended listening practices and interventions in aural perception.

But it would be naive for sonic artists to uncritically celebrate the new tools simply as means to further improve their bachelor machines. (And yet, were they unable to listen, could they ever truly obey?).

Regardless of how desirable some potential applications of listening technologies in sonic art contexts may be, artists cannot simply rely on scientists to explain and hence also define what listening is. It is important for artists to join the debate and consider the fundamental methodological differences between science and art and the possible implications any unreflected use of technology might have through inadvertently 'importing' implicit conceptualisations of listening into artistic practice. This is ever more important as any formalisation of human listening processes is always based on fundamental ideas about human perception and hence on human nature as such.

From the viewpoint of science, listening might at first glance be (and often enough still is) interpreted as dealing with the perception and interpretation of sound pressure waves. But listening is rather one form of human interaction with the environment as a whole. It is this quality of human listening that enables sonic art to be such a powerful medium for the exploration of human perception and interaction with our world. Especially in artistic contexts (and listening in any context can be this art), listening needs to be understood as a creative act and as such as an open-ended affair. Human listening is not simply the recognition of defined patterns in data retrieved from the outside world via our ear canals. It is not an acoustic land survey, but much rather an integration of the heard into individual horizons at positions not necessarily pre-determined.

---

9. Goto—an application to recognise chorus and replace bass-kick in mixes of pop songs.

As contemporary sound arts do not exhaust themselves in providing audible objects in time by making use of traditional musical instruments or loudspeakers, artists strive to create situations and experiences allowing listeners, these fellow artists, not only to explore their world aurally in novel ways but also to aim at suspending ingrained listening habits to expand and sharpen individual listening practice. It is with this focus on listening in mind that machine listening research can be seen as a provider of potentially powerful tools to sonic art practice, but additionally as a neighbouring, if methodologically rather distinct, discipline in the study of human listening in its multitude of contexts.

Peter Szendy

The Panacoustics
of Listening-In

In his *Cahiers/Notebooks*, in 1936–1937, Paul Valéry wrote down a
possible subject for a short story:

> Tale—f[or] children or other— / Finear; Justear—One can hear hair
> grow. The other one is experiencing an infinite number of *effects*
> from sound— / music rips him apart because he can perceive
> horrendous irregularities in what seems to be the most perfect
> performance, the purest sound for others / Same possible tale f[or]
> sight. The pilot; the expert in nuances; the clairvoyant just like the
> fencer who perceives the tiniest sign on the face of his opponent.
> / Or for touch, or taste. / Meaning the various acuities of a same
> sense and their extensive or fantastic implementations…

For Sight, for the sharp eye exercise, Valéry mentions trades or
activities in which visual hyperesthesia is specifically required: pilot,
fencer… For Finear or Justear, however, nothing of the kind: there is
only the general evocation of a hyperbolic auditory sensitivity able to
detect even the noise of capillary growth.

Yet one could name professions in which the acuity of the ears is
required. Those called 'golden ears' in French, for example, who are
listening to underwater sounds for strategic purposes. Or the doctor
who examines his patient with a degree of detail one can get an idea
of by reading the remarkable pages that Laënnec, inventor of the
technique of mediate auscultation through the stethoscope, devoted
to the description of what he was picking up. Or the spy, as portrayed
in countless novels and movies.

It is this last figure of hyperlistening that I would like to examine
briefly, guided by a few words written by Joyce to depict Earwicker,
the main character in *Finnegans Wake*: "Earwicker, that patternmind,
that paradigmatic ear, receptoretentive as his of Dionysius". What
would this Finear and his earwickedness be paradigmatic of? What
would he be a model of?

Dionysius' ear is a sort of cave located in Syracuse, whose Italian
nickname, *orecchio di Dionigi*, seems to originate from Caravaggio:

when he visited it in 1586, the painter compared its entry to a human ear. It is said that Dionysius, the tyrant of Syracuse, used it to detain his prisoners and spy on their conversations. Around 1780, Swinburne asserts in the notebooks he brought back from Sicily that it was "constructed intentionally for a prison, and a listening place". But a century before Swinburne, the Jesuit father Athanasius Kircher in his *Musurgia Universalis*, published in Rome in 1650, already used the mythical cave as a prime example of what he called "echotectonics", i.e. an architecture of echoes used for audio surveillance purposes. It is according to the same principle, he explained, that acoustic ducts were designed in palaces and buildings of any kind.

In 1787, in his famous letters on the *Panopticon*, Jeremy Bentham also referred to Dionysius' ear, the paradigm of a spy listening that Earwicker would be the heir of. Although he did so in order to make his invention stand out:

> I hope no critic of more learning than candour will do an inspection-house so much injustice as to compare it to *Dionysius' ear*. The object of that contrivance was, to know what prisoners said without their suspecting any such thing. The object of the inspection principle is directly the reverse: it is to make them not only *suspect*, but be *assured*, that whatever they do is known, even though that should not be the case. Detection is the object of the first: *prevention*, that of the latter. In the former case the ruling person is a spy; in the latter he is a monitor. The object of the first was to pry into the secret recesses of the heart; the latter, confining its attention to *overt acts*, leaves thoughts and fancies to their proper *ordinary*, the court *above*.

As Michel Foucault explained, the *panopticon* is based on the internalization of surveillance by the subjects: they *can* be watched *at all times*, even if they actually are not. For this internalization to be possible, it requires for those who see to not be seen: one must be led to *believe* that they are being permanently observed. However, in Bentham's times, this asymmetry—to see without being seen—could not be ensured for listening: the supervisor who pricked up his ears could also be heard. So much that Bentham, after considering a hearing extension of the *panopticon* with tin pipes ("a small *tin tube* might reach from each cell to the inspector's lodge", he wrote), had to give up the idea. He explained that "by means of this implement, the slightest whisper of the one might be heard by the other," so that one could not know who heard who…

We therefore had to wait for the 20th century and the asymmetry allowed by the invention of the microphone for the internalising of audio surveillance to generalise. Just think about Coppola's *The Conversation* (1974), the TV series *The Wire* (2002–2008) or the countless politico-media scandals since Echelon up to the current revelations about the functioning of *News of the World*, to understand that the descendants of Earwicker and Finear have glorious days ahead of them. We live in the era of what I called elsewhere *panacoustics*.

Translated by Valerie Vivancos

Dawn Scarfe

Listening Glasses

Listening Glasses are hollow spheres of glass with a small funnel-like opening at one side, which is inserted into the ear; and a circular aperture at the other, which is exposed to the air. Each glass it tuned to a particular musical tone,[1] and acoustically amplifies this tone

through sympathetic resonance.[2] Using such a glass, a listener can discover a musical tone in sound that might otherwise have been too quiet to be noticeable.

The design of the *Listening Glasses* emulates *Helmholtz resonators*: nineteenth century acoustic tools developed by German physicist Hermann von Helmholtz to study harmonic details in sound. Following the work of Ohm,[3] Helmholtz asserted that many sounds which appear to originate from one source, such as a single note on the piano, are actually 'compound tones' comprised of a number of 'partial tones'.[4] He made and employed a series of resonators in his efforts to prove the objective existence of these partial tones.

Studying Helmholtz's illustration of a glass resonator,[5] I became captivated by the thought that this elegant and fragile vessel might momentarily 'catch' subtle partial tones inside, amplifying them and allowing them to be held in the imagination. To my surprise, Helmholtz revealed that he had used the resonators to identify

1. The term tone is used throughout this essay to denote "a single sound of a definite, recognisable pitch." http://www.sfu.ca/sonic-studio/handbook/Tone.html accessed 7th July 2011.
2. For Helmholtz's definition of sympathetic resonance see 1954, 36.
3. Helmholtz acknowledges the influence of Ohm's law on his theory of hearing 1954, 33.
4. For Helmholtz's definition of compound and partial tones see 1954, pp.22–23.
5. 1954, p.43.

musical tones in 'noises' such as the whistling of the wind, the rattling of carriage wheels, and the splashing of water.[6] I imagined Helmholtz listening intently through a glass to the sound of his environment, and this notion fascinated me. I wondered whether I might discover musical tones in the sound around me, and resolved to make my own series of *Listening Glasses* to find out.

I asked scientific glassblower John Cowley to produce a prototype device using the measurements Helmholtz set out for his glass resonators.[7] Eager to try the instrument out, I put it to my ear whilst walking across a park between the glass workshop and my flat. At first I couldn't hear anything too remarkable. The sounds in my 'glass ear' seemed much the same as my other, open and unobstructed ear.[8] I learnt that in environments such as quiet parks I would have to be patient to hear any convincing resonance from the glass. I could hear a distinctive atmosphere, Aeolian in character, which gave rise to the feeling of being in a glassy tunnel.

Occasionally a mysterious trembling tone emerged from the glass, and now and again, a 'click' or 'pop' as my shoe caught stones in the grass. Then a plane passed by and at a certain point in its trajectory its sound caused the glass to resonate loudly. This had the strange effect of making the plane seem much closer than it had been, even though it was moving away from me. So I had found a *d'* in the sound from a plane, but what did I feel I had achieved in this experience? There was some appeal in detecting a 'musical' tone in an unlikely sound, but what I enjoyed most was the process of waiting for the glass to respond. I couldn't predict which sounds would produce interesting resonances, so I had to keep listening.

Using a glass to direct my ear to sound in the park, I became more aware of processes of listening and hearing and how they interacted: how the feeling of being immersed in the sensation of the audible blended with the urge to isolate and make sense of its various aspects, such as what had caused a sound, whether I should be alarmed by it, whether it was pleasant to listen to or not. I had thought that a resonator would make me listen analytically, focusing my attention on the possible occurrence of one tone. Instead I became more aware of how listening is distracted at the same time as it is directed. I like to think that while using a resonator to study the

6. 1954, p.44.
7. 1954, p.373.
8. Helmholtz recommended closing off one ear to enable concentration on the sound of the resonator in the other ear (see 1954, p.43.) Using the glass I left one ear open so that I could compare the sound of my two ears.

sound of the piano, Helmholtz's ear led him astray, calling him to the rustling and whistling of the wind in the trees.

Helmholtz proposed that the individual fibres of the auditory nerve in the inner ear functioned through sympathetic resonance, the same principle by which the resonators sound.[9] However, Helmholtz changed his mind about whether hearing partial tones in compound sound should be regarded as 'mere' sensation, or a more conceptually rigorous act of making sense of the audible.[10] The struggle Helmholtz had with this territory serves to highlight the difficulty in categorising aspects of auditory experience as active or passive, 'real' or illusory. We can use listening glasses to help our ears to identify partial tones in sound, but in listening through the glasses, our ears remain open to the unknown and unanticipated.

The *Listening Glasses* were first commissioned and exhibited as a tangible, audible and sculptural installation for the exhibition *Sound Escapes*, SPACE gallery, 2009. Gallery visitors were invited to use the glasses to listen to other works in the exhibition and ambient sound around and outside of the gallery.[11] I subsequently used the glasses to produce a series of binaural recordings which documented my own search for musical tones in the specific sounds that Helmholtz described (wind, water, and traffic) titled *Through the Listening Glasses*, 2010.[12] For the sound installation *Do You Hear What I Hear* in 2010[13] I used a series of differently tuned glasses to collect eight simultaneous recordings of road traffic. The resulting streams of audio were diffused though the eight channel loudspeaker system in the TONSPUR passageway in MuseumsQuartier, Vienna, Austria.

Selected references

Erlmann, Veit. 2010. *Reason and Resonance: A History of Modern Aurality*. New York: Zone Books.

Helmholtz, Hermann Ludwig Ferdinand von [1877]. 1954. *On The Sensations of Tone as a Physiological Basis For the Theory of Music*, second English edition of the fourth German edition, trans. A. J. Ellis. New York: Dover.

Scarfe, Dawn. 2010. 'Listening Glasses', *Performance Research*, Vol.15, No.3 (Routledge) pp.43–6.

9. See 1954, p.148.

10. This anomaly has been highlighted by Veit Erlmann, 2010: pp.236–7.

11. See Scarfe, 2010, pp.43–6.

12. *Through the Listening Glasses*, 2010 was exhibited at 'Sound Acts', University of Aarhus, Denmark 23rd to 25th September 2010. http://soundacts.au.dk/en/programme/ accessed 7th July 2011.

13. *Do You Hear What I Hear?* was produced for 'TONSPUR 36', MuseumsQuartier, Vienna, Austria, 23rd August to 27th November 2010. http://www.tonspur.at/w_36.html accessed 7th July 2011.

Jessica Cawley

Listening as Social and Solitary Experience: The Transmission of Irish Traditional Music Through Recordings

Throughout our musical lives, one of the most effective and crucial learning experiences is solely *listening* to music—a fact universal across all genres and cultures. Considering that Irish traditional music is predominantly transmitted aurally, it is not surprising that traditional musicians often stress the educational value of listening.[1] Remarkably, though, when I asked participating musicians if there was a prerequisite in becoming a traditional musician, the only definite answer was 'listening.' In contrast, formal training or being born into a musical family was not necessarily considered vital; instead, musicians emphasised the importance of consistent listening to a variety of styles.

Of course, there are several types of listening (such as purposive, attentive, distracted, unconscious, and passive listening[2]) and the experience of listening to live music-making significantly differs to that of recorded music.[3] Lucy Green argued that all forms of listening have educational benefits (2002: 24), although these benefits may differ in scope and type. Considering these broad issues associated with listening, this essay focuses on the social and solitary (private) ways recordings can be experienced.

1. This essay is based on current ethnographic research on the learning process in Irish traditional music (PhD, School of Music and Theatre, University College Cork, Ireland). I would like to thank the participating musicians for their invaluable assistance. This project was partially funded, with many thanks, by the Society for Musicology Ireland and the University College Cork. This essay was originally presented as an unpublished paper at the ICTM Ireland Conference in Derry/Londonderry (2011).
2. For a full discussion see Cook 2006; Firth 2003; Garfias 1985; Green 2002, 2008; Malm 1992.
3. Turino 2008.

Recordings provide multidimensional listening experiences. Firstly, some argue that recordings decontextualize the way we experience music.[4] In the past, listening required close contact with live musicians; recordings now distance listeners from performers, and therefore, can be viewed as an isolating or solitary experience. However, others argue that recordings are a vital aspect of enculturation—a social force imperative to the learning process.[5] Recordings have additional social dimensions since they can also connect listeners to a previous time or place. Both these perspectives are valid; therefore, I propose that listening to recordings can *simultaneously* be a social and solitary experience.

Although recordings can physically, visually, or emotionally distance the listener from performer, the opposite is also true; recordings have the ability to link musical communities over vast distances and bring people closer together. The Irish traditional music community is an international group of people bound together by musical, aesthetic, and cultural beliefs. As a traditional musician born outside Ireland, recordings were not only essential resources; they also provided a connection to the traditional community.

The experience of getting a new album was a significant and unique one. Irish traditional music was rarely stocked in mainstream music shops, and not yet common on the internet. So to collect new albums, I travelled 30 miles from my hometown of Manchester, New Hampshire (USA), to an Irish music shop run by Mary Lou and Charlie Clarke. My long visits with the Clarkes were important learning and social experiences; I would often stay for lunch and we'd discuss various groups, artists, albums and upcoming concerts in the area.[6]

The act of getting an album was a social experience, but so was listening to it in 'isolation' at home. Although alone in my room, the recordings made me feel more socially connected to Ireland and to the local traditional music scene. One of my first traditional CDs was Paddy Kennan and Tommy O'Sullivan's *The Long Grazing Acre*. Interestingly, hearing the album now reminds me of the woods of New Hampshire, not of images of Ireland as one might expect. This album brings me back to a particular time and place, real social

---

4. Cranitch 2006; Dibben 2003; Malm 1992; Ó Cainann 1993; O'Shea 2005; Sommers Smith 2001; Veblen 1991.

5. O'Shea 2005; Rice 1994.

6. Mary Lou is an American born singer, and Charlie is a native to County Cork. They have run their shop Ossian USA since 1993, and also host house concerts and sessions. I humbly thank them for their years of service to the New Hampshire music community, and their advice, kindness and friendship over the years.

memories are recalled, and in this way, listening to the recording is a specific social experience. Helen O'Shea—a traditional musician from Australia—commented on a similar phenomenon, while discussing the album *The All-Ireland Champions*:[7]

> My first experience of musical community began with hearing this recording, a gift from a fiddle-playing friend that became the wellspring and touchstone for musical gatherings…
> (O'Shea 2005: 77).

Unfortunately, many people do not have access to live traditional music on a daily basis—this applies to people in Ireland, as well as abroad. Regardless of the local music scene, recordings provide a distinctive opportunity to immerse oneself in the music. When this immersion becomes possible, learners are more likely to identify with traditional music on a socio-cultural level.

Additionally, how we experience a recording can change considerably over time. In America, I listened fanatically to Conal Ó Gráda's album *The Top of Coom* (an example of listening in isolation). However, for the past year, I've been playing alongside Conal in a weekly traditional music session in Cork City. Although the difference is subtle, my experience of listening to Conal's album has changed. I once praised the album purely in musical terms, but now the album is inextricably linked with actual social and musical memories I have of Conal.

Recordings can also transcend time, as they allow us to listen to long retired or deceased musicians.[8] For example, without recordings, no one in my generation would have experienced the music of Michael Coleman or the Beatles. One of the most influential, educational, and helpful albums in my collection is *Tunes for Practice* by the great fiddle player Seamus Creagh. I moved to Cork in 2009, sadly only one month before Seamus's untimely death. Although I never met him, I am inspired and impressed by the level of admiration people have for Seamus. Indeed, musicians in Cork still tell stories and play sets they associate with Creagh. For the past 18 months, I've been learning the fiddle, and *Tunes for Practice* has been my bible. On the double CD, Creagh slowly plays 69 traditional tunes for beginners to learn by ear.[9] Seamus's voice is also an important

7. Paddy Canny & P. J. Hayes, 1959.

8. Gracyk 1997: p.146.

9. *Tunes to Practice* is an educational project funded by the Arts Council of Ireland, and was recorded and produced locally in Cork.

feature, as he takes great care to introduce the tunes and their sources. Hearing his voice, ornamentations, and style, makes me feel like I am experiencing *something* of Seamus. Nothing can replace face-to-face interactions, but Seamus's influence—both musical and social—is still felt long after his passing.

In conclusion, recordings foster both solitary and social experiences, since they can simultaneously distance and connect listeners and performers. Recordings allow learners to hear and play along with other musicians in the privacy of their own homes— a solitary experience, with significant social aspects. Recordings provide unique listening experiences that significantly impact the transmission of Irish traditional music.

Selected references

Cook, Nicholas. 2006. 'Playing God: Creativity, analysis, and aesthetic inclusion' in *Musical Creativity: Multidisciplinary Research in Theory and Practice*, edited by Irène Deliège and Geraint A. Wiggins, pp.9–24. Hove and New York: Pychology Press.

Cranitch, Matt. 2006. 'Pádraig O'Keeffe and The Sliabh Luachra Fiddle Tradition' PhD thesis, University of Limerick.

Dibben, Nicola. 2003. 'Musical Materials, Perception, and Listening' in *The Cultural Study of Music: A Critical Introduction*, edited by Martin Clayton, Trevor Herbert, and Richard Middleton, pp.193–203. New York and London: Routledge.

Firth, Simon. 2003. 'Music and Everyday Life' in *The Cultural Study of Music: A Critical Introduction*, edited by Martin Clayton, Trevor Herbert, and Richard Middleton, pp.92–101. New York and London: Routledge.

Garfias, Robert. 1985. 'Music: Thinking Globally, Acting Locally' in *Becoming Human Through Music: The Wesleyan Symposium on the Perspectives of Social Anthropology in the Teaching and Learning of Music*, edited by Paul R. Lehman, William E. English and Gerard L. Knieter, pp.23–8. Reston: Music Educators National Conference.

Gracyk, Theodore. 1997. 'Listening to Music: Performances and Recordings' in *The Journal of Aesthetics and Art Criticism*, 55(2): p.139–150.

Green, Lucy. 2002. *How Popular Musicians Learn: A Way Ahead for Music Education*. Aldershot: Ashgate Publishing Company.

Green, Lucy. 2008. *Music, Informal Learning and the School: A New Classrooms Pedagogy*. Aldershot: Ashgate.

Malm, Krister. 1992. 'The Music Industry' in *Ethnomusicology: An Introduction*, edited by Helen Myers, pp.349–364. New York: MacMillan Press.

Ó Canainn, Tomás. 1993. *Traditional Music in Ireland*, 2nd ed. Cork: Ossian.

O'Shea, Helen. 2008. *The Making of Irish Traditional Music*. Cork: Cork University Press.

Rice, Timothy. 1994. *May it Fill Your Soul: Experiencing Bulgarian Music*. Chicago: University of Chicago Press.

Sommers Smith, Sally K. 2001. 'Irish Traditional Music in a Modern World' in *New Hibernia Review* 5(2): pp.111–125.

Turino, Thomas. 2008. *Music as Social Life: The Politics of Participation*. Chicago: University of Chicago Press.

Veblen, Kari. 1991. 'Perceptions of Change and Stability in the Transmission of Irish Traditional Music: An Examination of the Music Teacher's Role'. PhD thesis, University of Wisconsin, Madison.

Discography

Canny, Paddy and Hayes, P. J. 1959. *All-Ireland Champion*. Dublin: Dublin Records. LP.

Creagh, Seamus. 2009. *Tunes for Practice*. Dublin: Claddagh Records TUNESFORPRAC. Compact discs [2].

Keenan, Paddy and O'Sullivan, Tommy. 2001. *The Long Grazing Acre*. Nashville: Compass COM 4355. Compact disc.

Ó Gráda, Conal. 1990. *The Top of Coom*. Dublin: Claddagh Records CCF27CD. Compact disc.

Contributors

Brandon LaBelle is an artist, writer and theorist living in Berlin. His work addresses the relation of the public and the private, sociality and the narratives of everyday life, using sound, performance, text and sited constructions. His work has been presented at the Whitney Museum, NY; Image Music Text, London; Sonic Acts, Amsterdam; A/V Festival, Newcastle; MuseumsQuartier/ TONSPUR, Vienna; 7th Bienal do Mercosul, Porto Allegro; Casa Vecina, Mexico City; Netherlands Media Art Institute, Amsterdam and Ybakatu Gallery, Curitiba. He is the author of *Background Noise: Perspectives on Sound Art* (Continuum, 2006) and *Acoustic Territories: Sound Culture and Everyday Life* (Continuum, 2010). He is currently professor at the Bergen Academy of Art and Design, Norway.

Davide Tidoni has produced a variety of works investigating modes of listening and sound-space relations. These include site specific interventions, sound ethnography fieldwork and listening workshops. He has presented his work at the Barbican Centre, London; the Ars Electronica Festival, Linz; the Venice Architecture Biennale; the School of Humanities and Social Sciences, University of Exeter and RAUM, Bologna.

John Eacott is a jazz trumpeter and composer. In the 1980s he was a founder member of the anarchic jazz group Loose Tubes and orchestral director for post-industrial metal bashers Test Dept. Since the 1990s he has composed for TV, film and theatre including the influential 'Gormenghast' and the Royal Shakespeare Company's acclaimed 2012 production of 'Taming of the Shrew'. Following his PhD on generative music he has focused mainly on 'Flood Tide' which at the time of writing has just had its 11th performance on the river Orwell performed by musicians from schools in Ipswich. He lectures in popular music at Middlesex University and in sound art at London College of Communication.

David Hendy is Professor of Media History at the University of Sussex, and a former BBC producer. He wrote *Radio in the Global Age* (2000) and *Life on Air: a History of Radio Four* (2007), the latter winning the Longmans-History Today Book of the Year Award. He is a frequent contributor to radio. In 2010 he presented *Rewiring the Mind*, a five-part history of the modern media on BBC Radio 3. In 2013, he presented a thirty-part series for BBC Radio 4 on the history of sound and listening from the prehistoric era to the present-day, called *Noise: a Human History*.

Salomé Voegelin is the author of *Listening to Noise and Silence: Towards a Philosophy of Sound Art*, Continuum, NY, 2010. Other recent writing includes 'Epiphanies' in *The Wire* 324 and 'Ethics of Listening' in the *Journal of Sonic Studies*, 2012. In her blog soundwords.tumblr.com she writes about the experience of listening to the everyday. Most recently her work has been included in 'Being Honeyed—An exhibition of Sound(in)Art' at Soma Contemporary in Ireland. Voegelin is a Reader in Sound Arts and course director of the MA Sound Arts at the London College of Communication, University of the Arts London. www.salomevoegelin.net

Michael Chanan is a documentarist, writer and Professor of Film & Video at the University of Roehampton, who started out as a music critic and made his first films for BBC2 on musical subjects. He is the author of several books on the social history of music, as well as others on various aspects of cinema, including *The Politics of Documentary* (2007). His video blogs have appeared on the *New Statesman* and his latest video is *Three Short Films About Chile* (2011). He blogs at Putney Debater: www.putneydebater.com.

Volkmar Klien spent his childhood engulfed in Vienna's rich musical life with all its glorious traditions and ingrained rituals. He works in various areas of the audible

and occasionally inaudible arts, navigating the manifold links in-between the different modes of human perception, the spheres of presentation and the roles these play in the communal generation of meaning. He has held research positions at the Royal College of Arts in London, the Austrian Research Institute for Artificial Intelligence (OFAI) and the University for Music and Performing Arts Vienna, where he currently holds the position of senior lecturer in electronic music and media.
www.volkmarklien.com

Peter Szendy is Professor of Philosophy at the University of Paris Ouest Nanterre and musicological advisor for the concert programs at the Cité de la Musique. He also taught in the Music Department at the University of Strasbourg from 1998 to 2005 and is currently a Visiting Fellow in the Council of Humanities at Princeton University. He is the author of: *Hits: Philosophy in the Jukebox* (2012); *Kant chez les extraterrestres. Philosofictions cosmopolitiques* (2011); *Sur écoute. Esthétique de l'espionnage* (2007); *Listen: A History of Our Ears* (2007) and *Wonderland. La musique, recto verso* (2004 with Georges Aperghis) amongst others.

Dawn Scarfe uses site-specific installation, performance and field recording to ask us to re-think our impressions of our surroundings. She works with delicate materials such as resonating glass sculptures and small loudspeakers. Individual parts of her works are encouraged to respond to each other or enter into a dialogue with their environment. Recent exhibitions include Klinkende Stad Kortrijk, ZKM Karlsruhe, Q-O2 Brussels, ARTe SONoro Madrid, TONSPUR MuseumsQuartier Vienna, Bios Athens and 176 Zabludowicz Collection London.

Jessica Cawley studied music education and saxophone at the University of New Hampshire. She became interested in Irish traditional music while studying abroad in Galway and began learning the traditional flute in sessions in the Boston area. The flute soon became her primary instrument and passion. Living, studying, and performing in Ireland since 2007, she achieved an M.A. in Ethnomusicology (University of Limerick) and is currently completing her PhD thesis (University College Cork). With a background in music education and ethnomusicology, both her studies provide an interesting perspective of informal learning processes within Irish traditional music.

Introduction by Cathy Lane

Listening to Self and Other

"Every one of us as a human being needs to be listened to..."
So begins Jean de Dieu Basabose whose work mediating conflict
has brought together and started to heal the lives of many people
who were caught up in violence in Rwanda. The following series of
essays describes many aspects of what a listener or rather a skilled
listener might be, and what constitutes 'effective listening' in a
variety of different contexts. Nicola Triscott, also writing about
the reconciliation hearings in Rwanda, describes three stages,
those of listening, hearing and understanding, in the process of
conflict resolution. As an outsider and a foreigner she has played an
important role witnessing reconciliation hearings and events and,
as one who listens, hears and understands, she also records, tells
and retells the personal narratives that she has heard. For her in this
situation, listening is difficult and challenging. Polly Nash also writes
of her own discomfort at listening to the harrowing experiences of
others, in this case Omar Deghayes recounting aspects of his capture,
rendition and incarceration in Guantánamo Bay through his own
listening in circumstances where he was unable to see.

Who can be as important as *how*. We all need the right people to
engage in listening to us, people who are meant to hear rather than
who overhear. Social relations in populated spaces have long been
defined by who can hear what, and Niall Atkinson reminds us that
public spaces in Renaissance Florence were designed to safeguard
aspects of the privacy of its inhabitants so that even in wide open
public areas, private conversations could potentially be kept more
secret than they could in private rooms.

"Strive to understand. Engage all of your faculties, intellectual
and emotional." Diana Corley Schnapp's attribution of this as the
basis of the Jewish faith can also be said to form a basis to all
the articles in this section, articles which, one by one, struggle
to express what listening really is, reveal its difficulties and
yet remind us how essential it is for our moral, spiritual, and
intellectual welfare as both individuals and societies. Listening is
so much more than merely hearing, it is "attending, plus processing
physiologically, psychologically, and sociologically the messages".
In fact, true listening is so potentially profound, Lisbeth Lipari
reminds us, that it isn't just about acquiring new facts or information but should be able to result in a "kind of de-centring that
calls us to question or shed our old views and certainties about our
world".

So listening is not easy, it is something that requires full concentration and the engagement of all our faculties. It is also an attitude, a

state of mind, a way of being, something that happens inside as well as coming from the outside. It is, as Ansuman Biswas reminds us, a fundamental skill which involves the whole body and which has to be practised in order for us to improve. Biswas talks about the difference between the physical act of hearing and what it is to listen as something internal and spiritual. In Islam, as Kenneth Avery reminds us, the aural sense is primary in receiving and practising faith, and *sama* (audition or listening) is central to spiritual Islam. The *daf*, the Sufi drum, is part of the aural landscape of spiritual Islam, it organises the forces of the universe and calls Allah into the room, says Seth Ayyaz. In the performance situation that he describes in his meditation on listening as a biopsychosocial condition, it transcends its liturgical voice and becomes part of a different aural network—that of the five perfomers and the 'mind-brains' of the audience present at the performance of the Automatic Writing Circle in London's Swiss Church to combine their "multiple listening-histories, traditions and associations".

However, it is not only the voices of the unheard and the mute that we must focus our listening on but also the voices that are inside us… the inner voices that spiritual experiences across all religions have been built on. But can we still hear them? And, Daniel Smith asks, if we hear these internal voices, be they the voice of god, some other unrecognised part of our psyche or something else, should we say anything about them for risk of being labelled mad? Refuting these mysterious voices as being from outside ourselves and attributing them to hallucinogenic, clinically diagnosable psychosis results in a reduction in acceptable sensory experience and a whole world view of possibility.

Listening Others

A few years ago in Silsbee, Texas, a high school cheerleader refused to cheer for the high school basketball player who had raped her. When her assailant, who later pleaded guilty to the assault, went to the foul line for a shot, the cheerleaders began chanting his name. In protest, the young woman stepped back and sat silently on the bench. According to the newspaper, she said, "I didn't want to have to say his name, and I didn't want to cheer for him. I didn't want to encourage anything he was doing."[1] But when the school's principal ordered her to cheer for the player or quit the team, her family sued the school for infringing on her free speech rights, and for punishing her and not the player. The case eventually made it to the U.S. Fifth Circuit of Appeals, which ruled that the young woman's silence was not, in fact, protected speech. The eloquence of her silence was simply lost on them. They did not listen.

So many of our ideals about ethics and justice are centred upon speaking that we can wind up deaf or downright hostile to the silence of listening. Even the brilliantly innovative 1980s' AIDS activist organization ACT UP made its crucial political insight on the back of listening by using the slogan *silence=death*. In one sense it is certainly true that the silence around sexuality and HIV paved the way for untold tragedies of illness and death, but might we not also say that the *failure to listen=death?* Educators, judges, lawmakers and activists are not alone in their speech-centricity, however. For far too long our scholarship and social practices, be they in courtrooms or classrooms, or in town or union halls, have taken speech and speaking as stand-ins for *the logos*.[2] But a logos without listening is no logos at all.[3] When we fail to listen to others *as other*, we deny their alterity and limit our own horizons of meaning. But when we

1. Egelko, Bob. 'Texas Cheerleader Suing—Didn't Root for Attacker'. *San Francisco Chronicle*, November 5, 2010, SFGate.com edition, sec. A.

2. *Logos* is a Greek word that has for millennia been used, variously, to mean reason, rationality, discourse, word, knowledge, account, etc., but was perhaps never related to listening until Heidegger's reflections on Heraclitus in, Heidegger, M. *Early Greek Thinking*. New York: Harper & Row, 1950.

3. Fiumara, Gemma C. *The Other Side of Language: A Philosophy of Listening*. New York: Routledge. 1990.

listen to the other *as other,* we pave the way for an ethic that can *listen others to speech* and, in so doing, put our self-conceptions and dearly-held certainties at risk. By stepping off the cliff of ego-bound self-certainty, the communicative acrobatics of listening to others *as other* makes ethics and transformation (of selves, others, and even worlds) possible.

In the English language, many verbs have both transitive and intransitive uses wherein transitivity conveys agentive action of the subject, as in *she speaks the words* (transitive) and less so in *she speaks to him* (intransitive). In English, the verb *to hear* has transitive uses—we can say *she hears the voice,* whereas the verb *to listen* has only intransitive uses—we say *he heard the words* but not *he listened the words.*[4] Similarly, we say *she listens* or *she listens to the others,* but not *she listens the others.* In French, by contrast, both *écouter* and *entendre* are transitive verbs that can act directly upon an object, as in *je vous écoute* and *je t'entends.* The question of why the transitive form of *listen* has disappeared from English is beyond the scope of this essay, but it is worth examining the previously undisclosed meanings that emerge when we employ the verb *to listen* transitively. The feminist theologian Nelle Morton describes how *listening others to speech* is itself a political act. She writes, "we empower one another by hearing the other to speech. We empower the disinherited, the outsider…"[5] How resonant Morton's phrasing is here with Levinas' ethical response to the face of the "widow, the orphan, and the stranger" who "commands me as Master" from "a dimension of height."[6] The mutual empowerment of *listening others to speech* reverses authoritative normative social arrangements that silence and/or refuse *to listen the voices* of the oppressed. Transitive uses of the verb listening thus convey a sense of listening as constitutive of and prior to speaking—listening is an invocation, a calling forth of speech. The invocations of dialogic ethics give birth to speech by listening, by which we offer our hospitality to the other and the world. Thus it is not only that the voice of the other requires a listener to be complete; it is that without a listener, the speaking simply may not take place.

Another recent example of the kind of injustices that occur when our exclusive focus on speech drowns out the sound of listening

4. We are here building on the etymology of these words that suggest historical distinctions between hearing as a perceptual process of reception and listening as an attentional process of giving. For more on this see Lipari, Lisbeth. 'Listening Otherwise: The Voice of Ethics'. *International Journal of Listening* 23, no.1 (February 2009): pp.44–59.

5. Morton, Nelle. *The Journey Is Home.* Boston, Massachusetts: Beacon Press, 1985, p.128.

6. Levinas, Emmanuel. *Totality and Infinity: An Essay on Exteriority.* Translated by Alphonso Lingis. Pittsburgh: Duquesne University Press, 1969, pp.213–214.

is the recent U.S. Supreme Court case *Citizen's United v. Federal Election Commission*. In an attempt to regulate 'big money' campaign contributions, the Bipartisan Campaign Reform Act (BCRA) was passed by Congress and signed into law by President Bush in 2002. The law attempts to restrain some of the excesses of campaign advertising by applying a variety of restrictions to 'electioneering communications' (political ads and/or paid programming targeted to the electorate) transmitted 30 days (sometimes 60 days) prior to elections. In their ruling, the majority of the justices overturned BCRA, opening the door to a virtual tsunami of corporate funding. The majority justified their decision by maintaining that political speech is indispensable to a democracy. The question of whether, or to what extent, freedom of speech requires an equally passionate protection of listening and *the freedom to listen to others*, apparently never crossed their minds.

Perhaps because it is always so good to hear the voice of ethics speaking, we seem to rarely notice if anyone can, or does, listen. Or perhaps it's because listening is dangerous—to truly listen to the voice of ethics means we are drawn beyond the limits of our subjective understanding and knowing. *Listening others to speech* requires that our world change—that what we thought we knew or understood, or what we thought about how the world was shaped, what people were like, what was true, and so forth, are transformed. It's not about the acquisition of facts or information—our world doesn't necessarily change with new information. Our world only changes when there is a kind of de-centring that calls us to question or shed our old views and certainties about our world. For instance, when the Europeans discovered that their maps of the world were wrong and they encountered the North American continent rather than Asia, their world didn't change, really. Yes they identified new lands to exploit, but they still stayed at the centre of their world, their mission to conquer unquestioned; their view of themselves as righteous inheritors, emperors and missionaries didn't shift. They didn't shed their skin.

Listening others to speech is thus not a strategic or tactical practice aimed at achieving a predetermined goal, because that kind of instrumentality violates the alterity of others as well as the demands of present moment. Buber's observation that true dialogue is "a matter of renouncing the pan-technical mania or habit with its easy 'mastery' of every situation,"[7] is echoed by Levinas's insistence on

7. Buber, Martin. 1975. *Between Man and Man*. New York: Macmillan Publishing. p.39.
8. op. cit., p.206.

responsibility for the other, and on Morton's reflection that "clever techniques seen as positive agents for creation and change are not good for the kind of hearing that brings forth speech."[8] Thus, it is never a question of whether the voice of ethics speaks, because it is always speaking. The question is whether we are listening.

Selected references

Morton, Nelle. 1985. *The Journey Is Home*. Boston: Beacon Press.
Levinas, Emmanuel. 1968. *Totality or Infinity*. Pittsburgh: Duquesne University Press.

Diana Corley Schnapp

Spiritual Listening to Inner Messages: What Do We Know So Far?

Listening to God is a foundational belief in Jewish tradition. Chief Rabbi Lord Sacks of England (2011), a member of the House of Lords, defines listening as the keyword of Judaism in that *Shema*, "Hear, O Israel, the Lord our G–d, the Lord is One," forms the centre of the Jewish faith. He reasons that Judaism is based on *listening* to God rather than being able to *see* God. From the time of Moses, in all Torah examples of God's direct interaction with man or mankind, God hides his face from those with whom He communicates. People hear the *voice* of God or talk with an angel of the LORD but do not see the face of God directly (The Torah, 1981. See for example Exodus 3:1–6; Exodus 19:9; Exodus 24:17; Exodus 33:20). Sacks notes several forms of the word *Shema* to indicate the many ways one listens to God:

1. *u'shema* meaning "to pay attention" (Deuteronomy 27:9)
2. *shamati*, to hear, as in, "I heard and I was afraid." (Genesis 3:10)
3. *yishme'u* to understand, as in "Come let us go down and confuse their language so they will not understand each other." (Genesis 11:7)
4. to internalize, register, take to heart as was said about Ishmael, "I have taken into account what you have said." (Genesis 17:20)
5. *vayishma*, to respond in action, "Abraham did what Sarah said". (Genesis 16:2).

Sacks further asserts the power of listening as reflected in *Shema* by saying, "'*Shema Y'israel*' does not mean 'Hear, O Israel'. It means something like Listen. Concentrate. Give the word of G–d your most focused attention. Strive to understand. Engage all of your faculties, intellectual and emotional. ...In Judaism faith is a form of listening: to the song creation sings to its Creator, and to the message history delivers to those who strive to understand" (2011: 3). In sharing this view, Sacks encourages all Jews to listen actively in the same sense as listening scholars who have defined listening as attending, plus processing physiologically, psychologically, and sociologically the messages we hear (Wolvin, 2010). It is important to note that listening goes beyond hearing with the ear and registering sound on the brain. In listening to inner messages, the message may take a form that is not a physical sound. Sometimes the message is a feeling, an intuition, or a vision.

Rabbi Goldie Milgram (2011) encourages Jewish individuals to listen to God by *focusing* to hear the messages. She says the *bat kol* or echo of God's voice may be heard in stillness and quietness. She refers to Rev Kook, a 19th century chief Rabbi of Israel, who explained, "the soul is always communicating with us as our inner voice, our uniqueness, containing knowledge of our mission in life" (p.2). Milgram goes on to say that Rev Kook wrote that if one doesn't listen to her inner voice she will become depressed, personally confused and there will be a lack of passion. Thus Milgram adds more reasons for listening to inner messages: obtaining direction and assuring positive quality of life. Rabbi Aryeh Ben David offers an alternative view of listening to God: "Is God answering me? I would put it, God is always talking to me, but only occasionally do I listen" (p.77).

Christian writers also consider the reasons for listening to metaphysical voices. Fryling (2003) defines spiritual listening as paying attention to God. She asserts that listening to God is the heart of the gospel message and the goal in Christianity is to "listen more attentively to the voice of Jesus in Daily Life" (p.1). In her analysis of the listening process involved in this type of listening, the source is God, Holy Spirit or Jesus; the channel may be Scripture, prayer, or silence; the purpose is to discern the whispers of the Spirits in the midst of the noise of life. Christianity gives much attention to listening to God as well as to listening to the Holy Spirit, saints, and angels. The purposes of listening to Spirit include having a better life, receiving spiritual guidance, connecting to God, making decisions and learning to serve others. Fryling asserts that by listening to the prompting of God, a number of advantages may be gained: "to listen to God, to pay attention to the gentle whispers of the Holy Spirit directs us, heals us, helps us, and blesses us" (2003, p.68). Others are in agreement with the idea that listening to the inner spiritual messages results in helping us to endure the challenges of life, enjoy life, enrich the lives of others, and continue in spiritual growth (Dimartini, 2011; Stanley, 1985).

Other writers, including meditation and yoga teachers such as Kempton (2004), may not attribute the messages to God; but they also claim listening to the inner messages will improve quality of life. Kempton observes that if one slows down and listens to the body and feelings, "you soon begin to notice that helpful inner messages are coming to you all the time through sensations in the body, flashes of insight, intuitive feelings and even from that state of clarified intelligence that the Yogasutra calls *rtambara prajina*, or truth bearing insight" (p.1). McLaughlin (2011) of the Centre for Visionary Leadership is in agreement that a relatively pure spiritual seeker picks up clearer messages from the higher spiritual planes. She believes that "[i]f you are actively pursuing a spiritual path and a life of service and compassion and have worked on purifying your personality, then you may receive clearer guidance from your own soul or even higher levels than from someone else" (p.2). Lindahl (2003) calls this type of listening Reflective Listening, which she says is, "about listening inward, listening to our self—our True Self—getting to know the voice of our soul" (p.29).

Modern mystics seek deeper understanding of the outward life by tuning into the inner voices. Bean (2011), a teacher of Sant Mat Meditation and Surat Shabda Yoga, emphasises accessing the spiritual direction and wisdom that comes from within, a source of wisdom that not only provides an inner perception of bliss, insight, or affirms a 'Truth' of some sort, but also an inner intuition that can also make a positive contribution to one's outward life on the physical plane.

It would seem that the scientific examination of the context of religious/spiritual listening is particularly lacking (Corley Schnapp, 2010; Hedahl, 2001). The Research Committee of the International Listening Association called in a White Paper for formulation of theory and stronger qualitative and quantitative research on the subject of listening in all contexts. This view is echoed by Bodie (2011) and Bostrom (2011) in a special issue of *The International Journal of Listening*. Janusik (2007) is among those currently involved in building theory related to cognitive listening processes. Wolvin (2010) has assembled some current efforts at investigating listening from a broad perspective.

Among the relevant issues are: What constitutes listening in the spiritual attention to inner messages? Is there a distinction between spiritual inner message and intrapersonal communication; and, if so, how so do the listening skills we employ differ for each type of communication? Is it possible to ascertain the source of inner messages? What is the relationship between our reaction to inner voices and our interpersonal, intercultural, and/or small group communication?

The field is in the pioneer stages of such investigation.

Selected references

Bean, J. M. 2011. 'Contemplative Silence: The art of tapping into our source of inner wisdom and guidance'. http://www.innertapestry.org/columns/exploring-religion/627-contemplative-silence-the-art-of-tapping-into-our-source-of-inner-wisdom-and-guidance.html

Bodie, G. D. 2011. 'The understudied nature of listening in interpersonal communication: Introduction to a Special Issue'. *The International Journal of Listening*, 25 (2–3), pp.10–26.

Bostrom, R. N. 2011. 'Rethinking conceptual approaches to the study of "listening"'. *The International Journal of Listening*, 25 (2–3). pp.10–26.

Corley Schnapp, D. 2010. 'Listening in spirituality and religion'. In A. D. Wolvin (ed.), *Listening and Human Communication in the 21st Century*. London: Wiley-Blackwell. pp.239–265.

Fryling, A. 2003. *The art of spiritual listening: Responding to God's voice amid the noise of life.* Colorado Springs, Co: Shaw Books.

Grey-Cobb, M., & Grey-Cobb, G. 2008. *Angels the guardians of your destiny.* Huntsville, AR: Ozark Mountain Publishing.

Hedahl, S. K. 2001. *Listening ministry: Rethinking pastoral leadership.* Minneapolis, MN: Fortress Press.

Janusik, L. A. 2007. 'Building listening theory: The validation of the conversational listening span'. *Communication Studies*, 58(2). pp.139–156.

Kempton, S. 2004. 'Hearing inner guidance: How to find the wisdom that is always there'. in *Yoga Journal, September/October, 2004.*

Lindahl, K. 2002. *The Sacred Art of Listening.* Woodstock, VT: Skylight Publishing.

Lindahl, K. 2003. *Practicing the sacred art of listening: A guide to enrich your relationships and kindle your spiritual life.* Woodstock, VT: Skylight Publishing.

McLaughlin, C. 2011. *Evaluating spiritual guidance.* Retrieved from visionarylead.org/.../eval;-spiritual-guidance.html

Milgram, G. 2011. *Judaism and focusing techniques.* Retrieved from http://tinyurl.com/crlgoyo

NIV Study Bible. 1985. Grand Rapids, MI: Zondervan.

Research Committee International Listening Association. 2008. 'Priorities of listening research: Four interrelated initiatives' paper presented to the annual meeting of the International Listening Association.

Sacks, L. 2011. *Va'Etchanan: Meanings of Shema.* Retrieved from http://tinyurl.com/d3soov2

Stanley, C. 1985. *How to listen to God.* Nashville, TN: Thomas Nelson Publishers.

The Torah: A Modern Commentary. 1981. W. G. Platt (ed.). New York: Union of American Hebrew Commentary.

Wolvin, A. D. 2010. 'Listening engagement: intersecting theoretical perspectives' in *Listening and Communicating in the 21st Century* (pp.1–30), A. D. Wolvin (ed.). West Sussex, United Kingdom: Wiley-Blackwell.

Daniel Smith

One Must Be So Careful With Names

The story goes likes this: a shepherd was tending his flock on the side of a mountain in what is now central Greece when the Muses came down and spoke to him. "You shepherds of the wilderness", the Muses said, "poor fools, nothing but bellies,

> we know how to say many false things
>> that seem like true sayings,
> but we also know how to speak the truth
>> when we wish to."
>>> So they spoke, these mistresses of words,
>>> daughters of great Zeus,
> and they broke off and handed me a staff
>> of strong-growing
> olive shoot, a wonderful thing;
>> they breathed a voice into me,
> and power to sing the story of things
>> of the future, and things past.

This is how Hesiod's eighth-century B.C.E. *Theogony*, the earliest known genealogy of the Greek gods and one of the canonical texts of classical Greece, begins, with a moment of sudden inspiration —a moment of voice-hearing. One second, everything is normal, everything is regular, everything is mundane. The next second: the gods are speaking in your ears.

More than 2,700 years later, it is worth asking the question: Is such an experience still possible? Technically, which is to say biologically, it inarguably is. The human brain not only remains capable of producing what the philosophers George Graham and G. Lynn Stephens have called "alienated self-consciousness"—those eerie, sometimes terrifying instances when the notion "I say to myself" gives way to "I hear another speaking"—it remains prone to them. Over the past century, a number of surveys have been conducted to measure the rate of voice-hearing in the non-psychiatric population. One found that about forty percent of people have heard their thoughts spoken aloud at one time or another. Widen the net to include those odd experiences when, walking through a store or down a crowded street, you think you hear someone call your name aloud, and the number climbs to fifty-seven percent. Our minds, it should come as no surprise, are not wholly under our conscious control. Our senses often play tricks on us.

We can still hear voices, then. But is the experience still possible *culturally*? By this I mean: Is it still possible not only to hear voices but, as with Hesiod, to have the phenomenon accepted and even celebrated by our peers? This is the more important and ultimately the more troubling question. It's a question that also unveils a significant gap between how we and our ancestors have tended to conceive of unusual sensory experiences.

Aldous Huxley, perhaps the most famous champion of unusual experiences of the twentieth century, described this gap best, in a 1961 speech before a gathering of psychologists. "We now live in a period", Huxley said, "when people don't like to talk about these experiences. If you have these experiences, you keep your mouth shut for fear of being told to go to a psychoanalyst. In the past, when [they] were regarded as creditable, people talked about them. They did run, of course, a considerable risk because most [of these experiences] in the past were regarded as being inspired by the devil, but if you had the luck to convince your fellows that [your experiences] were divine, then you achieved a great deal of credit. But now... the case has altered and people don't like talking about these things" (Huxley, 1972).

There are exceptions to Huxley's thumbnail sketch, of course. During the 2004 American presidential elections, the popular televangelist Pat Robertson announced that God had told him that George W. Bush was going to win by a landslide (the Lord's polling data proved to be off by a wide margin), and Bush himself once reportedly told the Palestinian leader Mahmoud Abbas, "God told me to strike at al-Qaeda and I struck them, and then he instructed me to strike at Saddam". But these are the exceptions to the rule, and the rule is psychiatric. For all the neurological continuity between the age of prophets and saints and our own age, ask people what they think about when confronted with the words "hearing voices" and in return you will almost invariably receive an answer that is pat, definitive, and frightening: they think about insanity. Psychosis. Schizophrenia. Madness.

There are a number of sweeping, complex forces—political, intellectual, cultural, technological—behind this historical shift.

To my mind, however, the most profound force was a simple and seemingly modest alteration in how we talk about hearing voices. But, then, no change in how we talk about things is really modest. "One must be so careful with names," wrote Rilke, another great celebrant of unusual experiences, and the truth of his warning could not be clearer than in that moment, in the early nineteenth century, when the world's first psychiatrists sought to tame those experiences that had for centuries been thought of in a religious and artistic light by submitting them to precise medical terminology. In regard to what I have up until now been referring to as 'voices', we can pinpoint that moment with startling accuracy. In 1817, Jean-Etienne-Dominque Esquirol, one of the most prominent figures in the history of psychiatry, looked at the riot of words used to describe unusual sensory experiences—everything from 'locution' to 'revelation' to 'inspiration'—and decided that a single, universal term was needed. He decided on 'hallucination', and defined it as "the inward conviction of a presently perceived sensation at a moment when no external object capable of arousing this sensation is within the field of [the] senses" (cited in James, 1995).

Notice the clinical nullity of the language, the interpretative severity. When Hesiod stood with his flock on that mountain there was no "external object" stimulating his ear drums. There were, it is more than fair to say, no *real* Muses. Hesiod simply had the "inward conviction" that there were. What changes with Esquirol is the ability for that inward conviction to be smoothly accepted by others—for it to be socialised. Perhaps if Esquirol had been less prominent a medical authority, perhaps if the rising profession of psychiatry had been more circumspect or less zealous in its attempt to name the world of unusual human experience, the change in meaning would not have been so significant. But it was. From that moment on, you can watch as the word 'hallucination'—with its undeniably pathological connotation and gravity—grows in use and eminence, and you can watch as the capacity of people to choose for themselves what their voices mean lessens. You can almost hear the Muses dim.

Selected references

James, Tony. 1995. *Dream, Creativity, and Madness in Nineteenth-Century France*. Oxford: Clarendon Press.

Huxley, Aldous. 1972. 'Visionary Experience' in John White, ed., *The Highest State of Consciousness*. Garden City, N.Y.: Anchor.

Nicola Triscott

Attending Rwanda's Post-Genocide Reconciliation Workshops

Rwanda, a small nation in central Africa, is undertaking an extraordinary, almost inconceivable, social experiment: the reintegration of genocide perpetrators—murderers, rapists, and torturers—released from prison between 2003 and 2007, back into the communities where they committed their crimes, to live alongside their victims and their victims' families.

The Rwandan government is asking for reconciliation. More than this, it is a national policy. But how reasonable, how achievable is it to ask those who have suffered so much to forgive those who killed their relatives and children and destroyed their homes? And how realistic is it to expect those who were instructed by their leaders —government and church included—to kill friends and neighbours now to accept that what they did was profoundly wrong and to ask forgiveness?

Before I returned to Rwanda in January 2011, after a gap of eighteen years, I found it almost unimaginable that forgiveness and reconciliation could be possible after the genocide of 1994, during which more than eight hundred thousand people were killed in a hundred days, the fastest genocide in history, mostly hacked to death by members of their own communities. Far from understanding forgiveness, I felt anger that this should even be asked of people who had suffered so terribly.

I came back to Rwanda in order to see an old friend, a genocide survivor, whom I had met in Kigali in 1992. We had lost contact in the chaotic aftermath of the genocide. Unable to trace him for fourteen years, I thought perhaps he had died—of illness or the injuries he had sustained, but in June 2010, we found each other again via the internet.

As well as wanting to be with my friend again, I wanted to understand how the process of peace and reconciliation was working. My friend connected me with two remarkable men running organisations working for peace in Rwanda—Jean de Dieu Basabose who runs Shalom: Educating for Peace, who writes the companion piece in this volume, and Christophe Mbonyingabo of CARSA (Christian Action for Reconciliation and Social Assistance). Both men invited me to attend reconciliation workshops that they run with communities in Rwanda, in which listening to, hearing, and understanding are critical components.

Jean de Dieu is an intense and sincere man. He was a child during the genocide, surviving—as most Tutsi survivors did—by chance, and it has left deep psychological marks on him. We went together to visit the Gako community, to the north of Kigali among the hills, via a crowded minibus into central Kigali and then by long-distance bus out of the city. Jean de Dieu has been working with Gako community leaders and the local authority to develop a programme of reconciliation and conflict resolution. At the time, he was running some basic workshops with community leaders, but fundraising to enable a longer programme to include storytelling, songs and theatre.

The workshop he led took place in the open air, alongside a community building by the main road. A large group of around seventy people were gathered in this windy and slightly chilly place. Men sat on benches on one side, women on the other, mostly on the ground. Jean de Dieu told me that it was a mix of genocide perpetrators and victims/survivors, but that even he didn't know which was which.

The workshop was simple in structure, but extraordinary in this context where just seventeen years ago, neighbour drew machete on neighbour killing entire families of men, women and children. Jean de Dieu asked the people to stand up and hold hands in pairs, then in fours, then eights. They sat down in those groups to discuss the word 'conflict'. After this exercise, Jean de Dieu listened carefully to their conclusions and challenged them. No, he said, in response to one suggestion, you cannot avoid conflict. It is everywhere, but how you deal with conflict can make it a positive, 'cooperative' process. It was a sharing, listening process done with laughter and dialogue.

Jean de Dieu invited me to give a talk to the group, a request that startled me. I felt I had no special experience or wisdom to impart. But then I realised that to have an outsider there, listening to them, had significance beyond anything I could have anticipated. They expected me to have something of value to say to them.

Afterwards, Jean de Dieu and I, accompanied by some adults and the usual swarm of small children, went to visit the local genocide memorial, a simple structure set around a mass grave. I asked how many people were buried there. Perhaps 4,000 or 5,000, he said.

A few days later, I met the delightful Christophe Mbonyingabo of CARSA, a warm and friendly young man, who had come from the Congo to work for reconciliation in Rwanda. I accompanied him to a meeting organised by CARSA in a small community to the south of Kigali, where he and his colleagues have been working to bring about repentance and forgiveness between genocide perpetrators and victims and, astonishingly, directly between the killers and those whose families they had killed. I could not believe it was possible.

We arrived in the village, reached via bus and motorbike-taxi along unpaved roads, and entered a room in a low building in which around thirty people were present, seated on benches. I was asked to sit at the head table with Christophe and his colleague Sylvester. Christophe asked me to introduce myself, which I did, briefly telling the story of why I knew Rwanda, why I had returned and why I had come to hear what they had to say.

Those present were invited to give me their testimony. A woman stood up together with a man next to her. She told me that she had lost her seven children, her husband and her brother in the genocide. She told me how her children had died, hacked to death in front of her in a church, where the Tutsi community had gathered for safety, as she tried to protect them. She told of how she had also been "chopped" herself and badly injured. The man next to her, she said, was one of those who had killed her husband and brother. His brother had been one of the men who killed her children (he had since died in jail). She had forgiven them both. Now she said they were neighbours and that he helped her with her work. The man next to her then spoke, he said his goal was to be her good neighbour and that he tried to help her as much as possible, with errands and work, as she now had no one to help her.

A second pair stood up, two men. One told me that he had also lost his whole family, and that the man next to him was one of their killers. He had forgiven him.

Another man stood up and spoke. His family had all been killed when he was away. He had hidden in the fields and woods to survive. Next to him, one of his family's killers, a man in an orange shirt, spoke of his part in their killing with extraordinarily visual anguish, wringing his hands compulsively, his whole body twisting.

Did I want to ask any questions, Christophe asked. I asked the obvious question: How did those who had lost loved ones, especially the mother of seven, find it in their hearts to forgive?

The lady stood again, tall in her green skirt. She spoke of how she decided to forgive because that is what God teaches. She had come to forgiveness very quickly, even taking food to the killers when they were in prison. The man next to her, whom she had forgiven, was now like a good neighbour to her, helping her with her work, as she no longer had children or husband to help her.

I went over to her and hugged her (one of those gentle Rwandan embraces). As I turn, I found myself eye to eye with the man who had killed her family members and he took my hand gratefully. For a moment, I froze. But then I thought: if she has forgiven him, who am I to reject his repentance? So I held his hand and held his gaze.

Another lady then got to her feet. She told me that she had had eight children who were all killed. She told me the story of their killing in some detail, and of her survival. Unlike the other lady, she said she had found it very hard to forgive at first. She had lived in fear for many years, terrified every time she saw a machete or club. Then she had been appointed a magistrate at the local *Gacaca* courts. The magistrates had taken part in workshops that taught them about reconciliation and she had started to think about forgiveness. By the end of the *Gacaca* process, she had found she was able to forgive those who had repented. This, she said, had taken away her constant fear and she was more at peace.

The afternoon continued with more testimonies. A well-dressed man told me of praying for four days on his knees during the genocide, and receiving a "message from God" that he would not be killed. When the Interehamwe had attacked, he and the people he was with fought back. His companions were all killed. He was shot but hid and somehow survived.

I asked one of the killers what he thought of being told by one government that Tutsi were enemies and vermin and had to be extinguished, and by the next that what he had done was evil and wrong and had to be punished and repented. He spoke passionately in reply, mostly about God and the work of CARSA that had brought him to realise his wrongdoing. It was not an adequate reply, but how could it ever have been?

When I left, I went to embrace the people who had told me their stories of forgiveness. But no sooner had I embraced the woman who had lost her eight children than I found I was holding the hand of the man who helped to kill her family. It was a dilemma. How could I reject him when she did not? And then whom could I leave out? So I went around the room, offering my hand to each person, murderer or victim, known or unknown, and thanking them, and some embraced me in the Rwandan way.

When I gently hugged one of the survivors, one of the men who had lost his entire family, the murderer next to him—the anguished man in the orange shirt—embraced me fervently, almost crying.

When the gathering departed, I watched in astonishment as two killers and two survivors walked off down the dusty road together, apparently casually, as friends do.

It has been hard to know what to think of these workshops. Rwanda's experiment is complex, almost impossible, but they have no alternative. The problematics lie firstly in the lack of restorative justice. The survivors have had no compensation for their losses: the education lost by a child whose parents were murdered, the support in old age of a woman whose children were killed, the houses and livelihoods destroyed, the trauma and heartbreak that has ruined mental health. Most live in extreme poverty. I found that those groups organising reconciliation workshops understand that justice and economic rights go hand-in-hand, and the reconciliation process is often linked to direct acts of reparation by the perpetrators—the building of houses, helping with work, or the giving of gifts such as cows or fruit trees (provided through fundraising by the peace organisations).

Many have raised the paradox of the Church's complicity in the genocide with its role in reconciliation, but the groups I was with were independent of the structures of the Rwandan churches. (Why anyone would still believe in a god after the genocide is a question that perhaps only those of us educated to be aware of other belief systems can ask.)

I still do not think that forgiveness should be demanded, or even asked, of all survivors, and coexistence is a more realistic goal than reconciliation in Rwanda, certainly until this generation has passed. The revelation, however, that stays with me was seeing how receiving repentance and giving forgiveness had helped some survivors. It seemed to have helped them to find some sort of peace, and relieved their constant fear.

I came to understand better my role in these workshops, which had felt so uncomfortable at first. I represented the outside world, and as a *mzungu* (a foreign person or wealthy person) the 'developed' world, which during the genocide saved only its own kind and left Rwandan people to be slaughtered, doing nothing to intervene. I went to the workshops to listen and to try to understand, but in doing so I acquired a responsibility to the people I heard, that their stories should be recorded and told.

Jean de Dieu Basabose

Listening to People is Indispensible in Transforming Conflict

This article describes the role of listening in conflict resolution and community peace-building and will share experiences from fieldwork and point out some lessons learned.

Every one of us as a human being needs to be listened to.

From 2003 to 2006, I worked with a counselling and training organisation called El-zer Counselling Ministry. Essentially, my job was organising and facilitating training in counselling. Through this work, I understood how challenging it is to equip communities with skilled counsellors in the context of post-violent conflict. This context included, amongst other issues, recovery from war and genocide, floods of people returning from refugee camps, communities living in mistrust of one another, with suspicion and hate, and dealing with people returning from exile from different countries. Creating a 'safe space' where people can express their feelings, concerns, fears and hopes was the only successful strategy for effectively working with people in such a context. However, the space cannot be created without the active involvement of skilled listeners.

During the training sessions, we would hear participants revealing that their lives had been restored. It took me some time to understand this phenomenon: during the plenary sessions, emotions were aroused and many participants requested private listening sessions in the evening. As trainers and skilled listeners, we enthusiastically responded to such requests. What heartbreaking stories and living emotions were expressed when sitting in a confidential and comfortable environment, during this 'unofficial training program'! The participants were being effectively listened to. At the end of each training program, participants appreciated the training, expressed their restored hope and wanted to develop deep friendships with us.

This work with heartbroken people and divided communities stimulated my willingness to pursue peace studies so that I could contribute to preventing any re-occurrence of the terrible events that have characterised my country since 1959.

After my studies, I was challenged: I felt the responsibility to help communities to transform their daily conflicts in nonviolent ways. I took time to listen to myself and realised a possible and significant contribution I could make to a divided and traumatised society such as mine. But how could this be done? With which strategies? By what means? Who would support this? I needed someone to listen to me. Cori Wielenga, my colleague at the University of Kwazulu Natal's Conflict Resolution and Peace Studies programme, helped so much: she listened to me as we shared the same burden to educate our communities for peace and nonviolence. Eventually, we determined to co-found a peace education organization: Shalom Educating for Peace (SEP).

Listening to community members of Gako cell

SEP has initiated a Community Peacebuilding Project in Gako Cell. Gako Cell community is located in Rusiga Sector, Rulindo District, in the Northern Province of Rwanda. The community is making efforts to move towards socio-economic and cultural sustainability. The community, as is the case for the whole of Rwandan society, went through a very difficult period in 1994. Many Gako inhabitants were killed during the 1994 Genocide. A considerable number of the community members were refugees in the Democratic Republic of Congo and other neighbouring countries. Survivors of the genocide, relatives of those who perpetrated the genocide, the genocide perpetrators who were released in 2003, and others who are accomplishing important general labour as an alternative punishment are living in the same community and facing the challenge to embrace sustainable reconciliation and social cohesion.

To contribute to the process of building a prosperous, reconciled, healthier and peaceful community, SEP uses different approaches including storytelling as means of healing, interactive community dialogue sessions, and so on. Through dialogue sessions—where everyone is free to express their emotions—their ideas on how to rebuild the community, how to envision and shape the future of their community together, the community members clearly under- stood that reconciliation is possible. Before the dialogue sessions, the community members expressed the view that reconciliation would not be possible because of poverty; they thought that it would not be possible to move toward reconciliation if those who have to repair and pay back what they robbed or destroyed during the genocide did not fulfil their responsibilities. As they are poor and unable to find the financial and material resources required for reparation (as had been decided by the *Gacaca* court), the people assumed that reconciliation simply could not happen.

Yet SEP has created a space for dialogue where people listen to each others. As a result, people have changed their way of perceiving the process of reconciliation. Although they don't disagree with the idea of reparation, the community members now understand that reconciliation comes from forgiveness and repentance. They recognise that those two elements are very important (and not exclusive) to the process of reconciliation and are not 'buyable'. The people know that they may have money and repair what has been destroyed and yet not be able to repent. They know that they can feel unable to forgive others who have hurt them, even if they are able to repair what they have destroyed.

Lessons Learned

The following are some of the lessons learned in terms of the role of listening to people in conflict transformation and peace-building efforts while working with communities:

—Listening to people restores lives and creates a healing environment;

—As listening practitioners, we need to listen to ourselves and to be listened to as well;

—Listening to others can help in finding innovative solutions from which communities can benefit;

—Organising collective listening sessions can help in mitigating conflicts and enmity within communities, as it can allow others to know their fellow community members' stories;

—To move a human society towards sustainable reconciliation and social cohesion, the role of leaders with active listening skills is vital;

—Active listening plays an indispensable role when dealing with conflicts using collaborative approaches, such as those developed by SEP;

Jean de Dieu Basabose (with yellow green shirt), while working with youths (most of them were born in 1994—before, during or after the 1994 genocide) in Gako Cell during a listening session. The youths are sharing their fears and visions.

—Active listening affirms our respect of everyone in the community (children, youth, adults, poor, rich, illiterates, intellectuals etc.), a *sine qua non* condition for building a peaceful society;

—Active listening has a transformative power: to be able to educate people, we have to listen to them, begin from their knowledge and then build new understanding together.

Polly Nash

Listening to Stories from Guantánamo

In December 2008, while making a film about the US prison at
Guantánamo Bay, I went with journalist Andy Worthington and film
maker Mark Saunders of Spectacle to interview Omar Deghayes. Omar
was held at Guantánamo between 2002 and 2007 and this was the
first in-depth interview since his release almost exactly a year before.
When we met Omar, he had with him a pile of notebooks at his side,
notes of his memories he'd written since his release and return to the
UK, and said he wasn't sure that he would remember anything of any
use to us. Listening to Omar's story was the most incredibly moving
experience. The first few hours were less of an interview but more an
extraordinary stream of harrowing memories: of his abduction along
with his wife and baby by Pakistani authorities, his interviews with
British agents, being sold to the Americans, his rendition, torture
and abuse at their hands. There were times that I wished I wasn't in
the room. It was uncomfortable being a witness to his very raw and
surprisingly open revisiting of his experiences, hearing of things that
should never happen to anyone, and knowing that this was all done
with the full knowledge of our own authorities.

I have selected and very slightly edited two sections from five hours of recordings where I was particularly struck by his memories of sound; the first where he was not only blindfolded, but also had no knowledge of what was happening or going to happen to him, so had to build a picture of what was going on through sound; and the second, where sound and noise was a connection to life.

Transport Hood (Photo: PX Direct, suppliers to US Military)

From Pakistan to Afghanistan

One night, they took us to the airport and they handed us to the Americans... Suddenly there's Americans shouting, I'm in a place like an airport, I can hear the planes, and then suddenly the hood we had, the Pakistani hood, was taken off... to another worse hood than the first one, the first hood was very thin, and you could have some air. But it was a signal of a new, a real hardship... you could suffocate under there. I remember we were thrown on the plane, (deep sigh) and they used a rope and you can hear the "eek eek eek", you know something like that where the rope really pulls down, down, down, and you can feel it's going to cut you into pieces... it was used for planes or something... and you can hear people screaming "Ahhh" to stop those chains coming down... And the way they bunked us

Rendition Flight (Photo: US personnel private photograph)

on top of each other, it was really, really like you are moving furniture or something because you could feel somebody's leg is on your face and you're on the floor and you're chained like that and "eek eek" this thing, ropes are pulling you down and there was somebody next to me who was throwing up, inside this, (hood) imagine how horrible it was... And sometimes you get a kick from somewhere, and I don't know what, a boot comes from where, somebody's leg or feet will be in your face somewhere from one of those detainees and the plane got off and came down somewhere, I think it might have stopped somewhere, I don't know where, on the way to Bagram, stop and they collected more people, and "eek eek" and shouts again... and pictures, you can't imagine, I mean in this kind of condition there are some guards taking pictures, you know, "click click", you can hear pictures all over, and you can smell the alcohol and stuff, they have been drinking probably when they plane was going off, some guards and then we were sent down to Bagram and the new story starts from there. Bagram base, where all the other horrible stuff...

Guantánamo Bay—Camp Delta, cages and Camp Five isolation

Even those cages compared to Camp Five where I was moved afterwards, most of my four years were spent in Camp Five, I think those cages were like a paradise because there was air coming in, you could see the sun at least from the cages, sometimes we used to watch birds and used to really like that, we used to throw some food to them... you could speak to people because you are in the cage and some of the guys next to you in the cage that you see you could speak to them and speak to somebody from here though it was so noisy... It was fifty cages in one place and you imagine the noise and the chatting, and "dit dit dit" and the banging and if there was a fight or there is somebody ill or anything you can hear the banging and things

Camp Delta (Photos: Department of Defence/Global Security)

like this. It was like sleeping in the streets. ...those cages were better than the complete isolation where you can't see any light. You couldn't speak to anyone. If you want to speak you would shout, shout, shout so high there it was like you could make up three sentences and that's it. I mean it's better not to continue or else if so, somebody would come and bang on the door or something and you were obviously more tortured there, anything could happen to you because in cages you have always got

Camp Five Cell, 2007 (Photo: Joint Task Force Guantánamo/ Michael Billings)

Camp Five, 2008 (Photo: Joint Task Force Guantánamo)

people spitting in there and throwing on stuff, water and things like that. In isolation it is even more worse. It is only you alone and you are standing against everybody, guards and things like that. So it was a more horrible place. I mean I was four years in that isolation box.

Outside The Law: Stories from Guantanamo is a 75 minute documentary, directed by Polly Nash and Andy Worthington; Spectacle Productions, 2009. www.spectacle.co.uk

Kenneth Avery

Listening in the Sufi Islamic Tradition

Listen to the reed flute how it tells a tale,
lamenting its separation from the reed bed

These opening lines of the great Persian poet Rumi's masterwork, the *Mathnavi*, bid us to listen—to the melancholy music of the *nay* or reed flute, to its strange story of being parted from its home, the reed bed, a metaphor of the human spirit's separation from its divine abode and its lament at being left alienated in a foreign land. Rumi goes on to speak about the fire and the wind which is in this flute, how it plays its theme of love and longing for return, but how ultimately, when it has ceased its mournful song, it is the silence of the tongue and heart which speaks more eloquently of reunion with the Beloved.

This spiritual vision of Rumi expresses in elegant poetic form the role of hearing and listening, for in Islam the aural sense is primary in both receiving and practising faith. The muezzin's call to prayer from the minaret—though nowadays often performed with jarring loudspeakers—is the most obvious reminder of the presence of a faith community, and their obligation to pray. The sacred text of Islam, the Qur'an (a word which means literally 'the reciting'), is 'God's reciting', His speech, His eternal word. Because of this, it has always been primarily an audible text, heard, chanted and memorised, rather than a purely written scripture. The sonorous power of its recital in the original Arabic, a text which is part rhyme, part mellifluous prose, is difficult to overestimate. Believing that the Qur'an was transmitted aurally to the unlettered prophet Muhammad during the month of Ramadan, Muslims commemorate this event each year with nightly vigils of recitation and prayer.

For Sufis, the spiritual community of Islam, those who value the inner life of faith over the outward forms of religion, these recitations have evolved into the practice of *sama* (literally 'audition, listening'). *Sama* performance today takes many different forms in various parts of the Islamic world, with ritual chanting of prayers, poetry or invocations based on Qur'anic verses. It often involves musical accompaniment using a variety of locally popular instruments to complement the main focus on the voice of the singer/reciter. The mesmerising effects of repeated chanting or rhythmic accompaniment such as *tabla* drumming can evoke altered states or hypnotic trance in listeners and performers alike. These effects are familiar in a variety of religious and cultural settings worldwide, and psychologists are now beginning to understand them from a neurological point of view.

For the Sufis and mystics of other traditions, however, such altered states have historically been experienced as transitions of consciousness from the everyday waking state of alienation to the God-intoxicated state of 'nearness' (Arabic *qurb*) or 'presence' (*hudur*). Indeed, for many early Sufis in the first four centuries after the inauguration of Islam, God-intoxication and the cultivation of altered states was highly valued. These founding masters sought to alter consciousness, annulling the sense of ego-separation, fostering the sense of wholeness and oneness by constant prayer and fasting, and maintaining a prepared mind susceptible to inspiration.

Some devotees, like Nuri, a Baghdad Sufi of the late ninth century, cultivated such states that the least auditory cue, like overhearing a verse of poetry or Qur'an recital, could trigger a trance-like state. The biographies which mention Nuri, for example, speak of his love of poetry and his ready transition to altered consciousness. It is even said that he ended his life in this way, by injuries to his feet and legs from sharp canes when he danced all night in a thicket whilst in a hypnotic trance.

There is, though, another side to Sufi *sama* than the excesses of trance states. The Arabic verbal root s-m- carries the meaning 'to hear', but unlike most European languages, the senses of listening, hearkening and obeying are also conveyed in this linguistic root. This is best illustrated by a key Qur'anic text (chapter 7, verse 172) which became a fundamental tenet of Sufi thought. In this verse God speaks of the primeval covenant made with the future children of Adam, how they swore obedience and loyalty to Him. Their assent to His lordship is imprinted on all human souls, and for Sufis the affirmation of Islam is the fulfilment of this covenant: when they hear His voice they obey and confirm His will for them.

While hearing and obeying is an essential of Islam from the human point of view, the remainder of the created world also shares in devotion to the one God. For the poets, especially those who wrote in Persian such as Attar and Rumi, the motion of atoms, like motes in a sunbeam, is their way of praising and dancing to the divine.

Likewise, the movement of the stars and planets in relation to the sun mirrors the earthly journey of devotees toward their Beloved One.

The famous 'whirling dervishes' of Konya perform their dance in imitation of the movement of the planets around the sun. This Sufi order is descended from Rumi's time, and it is said that he composed his wondrous poetry in a trance state revolving around a pillar of his house. But despite the reciting and dancing associated with his poetry, Rumi's spiritual quest was an inner journey where the 'sound' of silence was heard. He wrote many thousands of short poems, as well as a massive 25,000 verse epic, the *Mathnavi* mentioned above. Yet paradoxically for such a prolific writer, at the end of his shorter poems he often bids the listener/reader *khamush* 'silence!' This is not only the poet silencing both the author himself and the reciter at the completion of the poem, but an invocation of silence in the heart of the listener. It is that silence which leads us on the transcendental journey in quest of peace and wholeness (the Arabic root of the word Islam s-l-m conveying these two meanings), a journey to the ineffable mystery of Life and Being.

Selected references

Avery, K. S. 2004. *A Psychology of Early Sufi Sama: Listening and Altered States*. Abingdon and New York: Routledge Curzon.

Lewis, F. D. 2008. *Rumi: Past and Present, East and West*. Oxford: Oneworld.

Rumi. 2004. *The Masnavi*. Translated by J. A. Mojaddedi. Oxford: O.U.P.

The Rough Guide to Sufi Music. 2001. RGNET 1064 CD.

Seth Ayyaz Bhunnoo

In the Midst of It All, Something is Stirring: The Biopsychosocial Condition of Listening

In the resonant church, in the midst of it all, a hush falls. Something is stirring. Void or plenum? A nothing, a beginning. Within the body of the Swiss Church in London in June 2011,[1] five bodies of the Automatic Writing Circle[2] are arranged, within the mind-brains of the audience. We are multiple listening-histories, traditions and associations; beings composed of discreet biological bodies, porous psychological bodies and diffuse social bodies. As systems of regularities and relations, we are also bodies in their most abstracted form, with the capacity to affect, and to be affected.[3]

The ensuing sound is a transduction of acoustic energy into patterned neural activity; contracting the reservoir of noise, the total sonic field around us, and expanding into the phenomenal experience of listening. We can narrativise the sonic in any number of ways—but there is a gap between the experience itself, and the language by which we articulate it. It is across this gap that mentalized sound operates.

My biopsychosocial approach to the condition of listening seeks

1. A recording of the performance can be found at http://soundcloud.com/seth-ayyaz/automatic-writing-circle-live

2. Automatic Writing Circle (www.automaticwritingcircle.co.uk) is an ensemble that maps resonances across bodies (Daf, Nay, Baroque Flute, Cello, and Ouija board—a multi-player instrument that uses technologies of recording, transformation and redistribution into a multi-speaker array). AWC are from diverse musical backgrounds, amongst them, historically-informed performance, noise musics, electroacoustic composition, experimental and popular music. We meet to explore the nature of these traditions, the currents that flow between them, and to experience the loss and rediscovery of sonic identity in the Ouija mediated composition-improvisation. Based on the real-time video analysis of the shadows cast by the hands of the performers, it reframes many of the conventions of traditional, tactile instrumental control.

3. "When a body 'encounters' another body, or an idea another idea, it happens that the two form a more powerful whole, and sometimes one decomposes the other, destroying the cohesion of its parts. In this way we come to relate to foreign bodies differently in the anticipation of their affects on our body." (Gilles Deleuze. 1990. p.19)

to ground narrativisation, thinking through how different levels of organisation cohere. Extending from Maurice Merleau-Ponty's circularity of embodiment, this entails considering the relationships between the biological (physical), the psychological (conscious and unconscious mental states) and the social (the supra-individual, transgenerational structures of history and culture). Listening is an extensible capacity of mind, constituted at all three registers. Highly complex neurodynamic states interact within sensorimotor loops, activated by the biosystem and its context, and are sustained for a certain time. In other words, we are systems that generate the intentional content of their listening states by "pulsating into their causal interaction space" (Metzinger, 2004: 21), transgressing discrete physical boundaries and so extracting information from the environment. Listening is a kind of ingesting that pulsates; we transparently hear-out through our neural apparatus, the machinations of which we remain largely unaware. It is the singularity of configurations of intensities playing across all three domains that gives force to the sonic body of any particular musical experience.

In the church before starting, I was asked: will you begin with the *daf*? That afternoon the discussion was to begin with a four-channel diffusion of synthetic particles, nebulae forming and dispersing. Now a deviation. Perhaps. But *daf* is the Sufi drum that organises the forces of the universe, calling Allah into the room. Different gestural agency, different kind of body, but resonating coherently at the conceptual level. Echoes of temporal and cultural displacement.

So, a beginning. The *daf* sounds an Islamic resonance, filling the church. A liturgical voice, somehow a-cultural appears from nobody. The Ouija instrument interjects a transformed sample, from only a moment ago, rupturing the smooth surface. The rhythmic ground reconstitutes into rapid pulses, draped by smeared acousmata. There is a melancholy, a haunted space, increasingly displaced by a vibrating *daf* skin exceeding human gestural agency, a long motoric vibration. The pulsating bodies of the AWC create a sonic body that fluctuates and flexes. A *fortissimo* cello reminiscent of Bach elicits a flurrying flute from on high, accompanied by birds. The bird-flute-cello is insistent and impatient, and then is gone. Later, I am playing a descending melody. Very slowly. It is my body, but it was not my conscious intention. Thought insertion. Made action. Made feeling. The baroque flute is doing the same, and the cello. It is a 17th century chorale from Jacob van Eyk. Bach may have used it too. We had played it earlier, with the thought it might be used, but somehow, the performance has determined it at this moment. My agentive self, the

"I" that causes my actions, has been taken over by an emergent non-self mind. An unnerving and exhilarating collapsed subject-object.

A shared interiority of mental states (a thought plus a feeling) has been transmitted via the sonic body of the performer-listeners. What Wilfred Bion (Bion, 1962: 6–7) described as ß–elements are diffused throughout, as fragments of activated proto-mental phenomena. An accretion of gestures, desires and implications, affectively charged, crystallise an immaterial sonic form, as this moment; extending from somewhere to now, jumping from one body to another, and enacted.

Music is sound organised either through human agency at the level of production, or by attentional focus, hearing sound as music. We are innately disposed to respond to music as if intentionality resides within it. We attribute motives, intentions, mental states, emotions, desires and moods to the sound, as if it bares the intentions of the producer. Musical listening is an exploratory capacity of a sonic mind mentalizing a sonic world, where mentalization (what Peter Fonagy (1991) proposes as "holding the mind in mind") affords the possibility of enacting music as if it were an other, an agentive interlocutor. Our listening is sensitised to the salience of anomalous sound which bears the marks of tooling.

The acoustic signal and its context couples with listeners to form a sonic body. This sonic body is constituted via cochlear hearing (the spectrotemporal patterning of acoustic energy) and also via visceral hearing (the affective effects on viscero-motor centres) in the context of other perceptual modalities. It takes in the implicative field of the sounds—what they might do or mean—to create internal events in the physical body. These are encoded and interpreted by an array of brain-stem structures, with auditory scene analysis being complete at primary and associated auditory cortices. From there it is mentalized, ramifying through the structures that form networks of associative meaning and our capacities for social cognition. These will in part be shared between mind-brains, and in part be entirely private, expanded by the individual listener's perceptual and personal histories. These histories are themselves situated in time, place and culture.

Music is a relational and social entity; understood as mentalized sound, it relies on our abilities of interpersonal interpretation. Mentalization (Fonagy, P. et al, 2002) is critically engaged in attentional control, affect regulation, effortful control, the agentive self, imagination and social cognition. Mentalizing mode entails (implicitly or explicitly) an awareness of the mind's intention or 'aboutness' (Leslie, 1987). Neurobiologically (Lieberman, 2007) we can differentiate an X–system for refleXively, automatically and affectively sensing and responding to the social world, likely subserving states of flow (Csíkszentmihályi, 1990), of losing one's self in the processes of listening and responding. There is also a C-system for refleCtive, linguistic, controlled, explicit and conscious appraisal of that world. In addition, there is a system of 'interiority', of mental states, which is independent of self/other. It is more a shared interiority of intentional-desiring-motivated-appetites and a system of 'exteriority' that senses the material world.

The forces that music brings are reflexive and reflective, implicit and explicit, interior and exterior. The force of its potentials is what animates the aesthetically-tuned sensorium. Composers, working with the contingencies of matter and sound, mentalize beyond language, imaginatively tracing the coupling of bodies and sensoria into aesthetic experience. In the production of new musics, it is the exploration of the uncertainties of how these forces will play out that is compelling. The composer-musician, in attending to her internal state of being when musicking, offers a potential transmission of that state to the listener. One can never know the exact experience of an other, but there is sufficient shared experience that we can talk as though we do—to be moved to tears by a singer, impassioned to action by a beat, subdued by a melody. Music then operates as a mental state attractor organising the aesthetically-tuned sensorium of the listener. The sonic body has activity and the power to move. In short it does something, inducing states of absorption and engagement, holding the listener in a modality of aural contemplation.

Selected references

Bion, W. R. 1962. 'A theory of thinking'. *International Journal of Psycho-Analysis*. 43.

Csíkszentmihályi, M. 1990. *Flow: The Psychology of Optimal Experience*. New York: Harper and Row.

Deleuze, G. 1988. *Spinoza; Practical Philosophy*. San Francisco: City Lights Books.

Fonagy, F. 1991. 'Thinking about thinking: Some clinical and theoretical considerations in the treatment of a borderline patient'. *International Journal of Psycho-Analysis*, 76, pp.39–44.

Fonagy, P., Gyorgy, G., Jurist, E. L. and Target, M. 2002. *Affect Regulation, Mentalization, and the Development of the Self*. London: Karnac Books.

Leslie, A. M., 1987. 'Pretense and representation: the origins of "theory of mind"'. *Psychological Review*, 94, pp.412–426.

Lieberman, M. D., 2007. 'Social Cognitive Neuroscience: A Review of Core Processes'. *Annual Review of Psychology*, 58, pp.259–89.

Merleau-Ponty, M., 2003. *Phenomenology of Perception*. Routledge.

Metzinger, T. 2004. *Being No One The Self-Model Theory of Subjectivity*. Cambridge, Mass: MIT Press.

The Automatic Writing Circle presented by CRiSAP (Creative Research into Sound Arts Practice) Sound Art at the Swiss Church in London, on 9th June 2011 (Seth Ayyaz, Peter Coyte, Kirsten Edwards, Thomas Gardner, Stephen Preston). http://soundcloud.com/seth-ayyaz/automatic-writing-circle-live

Niall Atkinson

A Guide to Listening to Renaissance Florence

What was at stake in listening in the pre-modern city? Let us take, by way of example, the diaries of two Florentine merchants for what they say about the importance of listening in a city whose social relations were defined not only by what one saw but also by what one heard. The first, written some time in the 1360s, is Paolo da Certaldo's (c.1320–1370) so-called *Libro dei buoni costumi*, which functioned as a kind of familial guide to successful living.[1] In it, he instructed his readers in the social, moral, and business practices that were typical of the values of an emerging modern bourgeois class. An important part of such practices was the careful control of the flow of information through the city's communicative networks, and as a result, he took detailed account of the lively interchange in streets and squares through a lens of moral anxiety. He demonstrated an acute awareness that one's actions and words were let loose in streets and squares where they began to circulate in a domain accessible to everyone, and were divorced completely from one's attempts to control them. As a merchant Paolo was extremely concerned with secrets and how to keep them while carrying out business in the hazardous acoustics of the public domain. He was less interested in how one constructed a personal façade vis-à-vis others than in analysing how information moved across boundaries and within certain spaces, all of which were traversed by competing forces.

Paolo cautioned his readers to be aware that when one spoke in public, there was always a chance that people were secretly hiding behind bushes, lurking around corners, or listening behind walls.[2] In a city like Florence, whose narrow, paved streets and countless street corners, along with its stone and plaster façades, actually diminished the range of one's sight while amplifying the range of one's voice, careful manipulation of the auditory sphere was a critical practice. "And similarly, if you enter a room", Paolo warned, "do

1. Certaldo. 1986. p.74
2. Ibid.

not talk or say anything if you do not know for certain who is in the room, in case there is someone behind a curtain or hidden elsewhere, who could hear the things you say."[3] He goes on to advise his readers to "make sure that you do not say things along a street, or at the intersection of a road, or by a thin wall, that you do not want anyone to know."[4] Secret things, therefore, had to be uttered softly behind a very thick wall. But since walls inevitably spring leaks, Paolo also proposed telling secrets right in the middle of the open square. "If you want to speak about secret things, say them softly, in a place where you are far away from any wall, so that you will be aware that your speech (*favellare*) will not be heard beyond the closest wall."[5] He knew that one was always subject to the watchful gaze of others, and that even the most quotidian spaces were charged with the volatility of misapprehension. However, it was out in the open that secrets, paradoxically, could be revealed because one had a clear view of any enemies who might be listening within audible range (Certaldo 1986).[6] This was the place of discourse, facilitated by the public benches that ringed the city's main square, the Piazza della Signoria. It was precisely the public transparency of the piazza that allowed Paolo to win back a certain domain of privacy and security from the enemies that haunted him. Clear sightlines and orderly spaces were not, first and foremost, aspects of a beautiful city, but necessary elements of a nervous and anxious one. One can deduce from his writing that the city was a network of contested zones where information was, on the one hand, the prize of the resourceful, and on the other, a potential weapon to wield or an asset to sell.

Paolo was grappling with the ambivalent nature of walls and spaces, seeing in them various degrees of porosity and opacity. He interrogated the ways in which walls could hide, but also reveal, while at the same time *spaces* rendered visible a variety of points of view even as they allowed secrets to be controlled and hidden. Walls were barriers to some, ways of accessing information to others. In short, their functions were fluid and ambivalent. One had to be constantly aware of one's relative position in space, in a system of relations with other interested and implicated parties, in order to

3. Ibid. "E simile, s'entrassi in una camera, non favellare e non dire niuna cosa se prima non sai bene certamente che è ne le detta camera, però che dopo la cortina o in altro nascoso, ch'udrebbero i tuoi fatti e detti."
4. Ibid. "Ancora ti guarda di non dire cosa lungo la via o lungo parete d'assi o di sottile muro, che tu non voglia che ogni uomo il sappia"
5. Certaldo. 1986. p.74 "Se vuo' parlare cose celate, dì piano, in luogo che tu abbi tanto largo di mura, che t'avvisi che 'l tuo favellare non sia udito fuori del più pressimano muro…"
6. Ibid.

determine just how a certain space or wall would contain, transform or redirect the meaning of one's actions and words.

For the wool merchant Giovanni Morelli (1371–1444), on the other hand, the piazza no longer provided a robust setting for open social and political confrontation. Therefore, in his diary, he withdrew into a reconstructed private refuge based on the topography of local social relations and the construction of a mute moral façade in open places.[7] Transforming the city's careful demarcation of proper limits and borders into a personalised itinerary, Morelli drew his own social map within the official boundaries of the city's legal construction of public space. Therefore, he instructed his family to acquire friends in the immediate neighbourhood for whom one could do favours.[8] He advised honouring them with dinner invitations, always having at hand some cool dry wine on a hot day, or a variety of good vintages to offer them on feast days.[9] In pursuing a young woman, he writes, "go to her neighbourhood at a proper hour;" that is, after one's shop was closed. "Do not go alone", he continues, "but with trusted friends, and make your virtue known to her *indirectly through the gossip and reports of others.*"[10] Therefore, his readers were counselled to coordinate, through their actions in public space, what others heard about them, which was, quite simply, the core of their public identity.[11]

Morelli demonstrated the multiple topographies that could be over-laid onto the city. Consequently, outside one's local neighbourhood lay an alien territory, where one's comportment was to be of a more dissembling nature as one navigated the contentious sites of oral exchange. One was to obey, follow, and not speak badly of Florence's sitting magistrates, even if they might be dishonourable in charac-ter. And although he heard rumours circulating through the city's streets, instead of tuning in, he advised his readers to simply tune out. He recommended silence unless one was ready to utter words of commendation, deafness against the seditious words of others, and

7. Giovanni Morelli. 'Ricordi.' In *Mercanti scrittori: ricordi nella firenze tra medioevo e rinascimento,* edited by Vittore Branca. Milano: Rusconi, 1986. pp.101–339.

8. Morelli. 1969. p.253.

9. Ibid., pp.260–61.

10. "…vavvi all'ore compitenti, quando se' uscito da bottega. Abbi uno compagnone fidato che faccia compagnia volentieri; piglia dimestichezza nella sua vicinanza con persone da bene; sia costumato e piacevole, usa cortesia con que' giovani suoi vicini; fa cotai operazioni virtuose e che a lei sieno rapporte…" (emphasis added) Ibid. p.261

11. Reputation was everything to a Florentine but such carefully constructed neighborly relations could also be used to one's benefit. In one of his novelle, Sermini recounts how a woman circulates the information around the neighborhood that she is related to her love interest so that they can legitimately be seen together. See Sermini 1874, 2, 573ff

refutation of any criticisms of the ruling regime.[12] Since there were a lot of nasty people in Florence, he declares, he counselled his readers to simply speak well of everyone.[13]

In contrast to the intimate comforts of the neighbourhood corner, Morelli also exhibits an intense apprehension about the way in which social discourses were let loose into public spaces. Outside one's neighbourhood, little capacity existed to control the circulation of verbal exchanges, so he advocated an alert façade of amicability, a surface of consensus and good-natured gullibility. To combat the deceitful, he proposed another kind of deceit, aware, perhaps, that speaking and listening in the urban environment produced unstable games of meaning in which each utterance was ripe for misunderstanding. Leaving the familiarity of one's neighbourhood was crossing into an unknown territory because it was never certain what could be said there, what needed to be kept quiet, how one needed to act in order to maintain one's sense of self in the absence of the familiar sounds of one's local neighbourhood.

Giovanni Morelli may seem to have internalised his own subjection to authority and Paolo da Certaldo may appear on the verge of paranoia. However, Morelli was also pragmatically trying to deal with the social façades that people always constructed in the face of the inevitable uncertainty of daily face-to-face relations. Negotiating space for him meant developing a mask that was impenetrable to those who traversed the city in search of information, stories, and secrets. The image we get of the everyday spaces of the city is not one of the free exchange of ideas. These texts do not depict a transparent, coherent picture of urban life. These city spaces were a series of highly contested aural zones, fluid in meaning, unstable from one moment to the next. The city as an acoustic space was not a harmonious chorus of voices, but dissonant series of both random and staged oral encounters, endless connections and possibilities that had to be constantly accounted for, anticipated, or circumscribed by those whose very livelihood depended on it.

Selected references

Certaldo, Paolo da. 1986. 'Libro Di Buoni Costumi'. In *Mercanti scrittori: ricordi nella Firenze tra medioevo e rinascimento*, edited by Vittore Branca, lxxxviii. Milano: Rusconi. p.603.

Morelli, Giovanni. 'Ricordi'. 1986. In *Mercanti scrittori: ricordi nella Firenze tra medioevo e rinascimento*, edited by Vittore Branca. Milano: Rusconi. pp.101–339.

12. That this was as much practical as moral advice may be intuited from a provision that made by the government in 1394 that encouraged secret denunciations of any defamatory messages posted in the city by offering 400 florins as a reward.
13. Morelli. 1969. p.275

Listening as Feeling

Why listening? Listening is a fundamental skill.

What is fundamental about it is not the sound, but the attitude. Sound does not lead to listening but listening to sound. To fixate on sound is to get caught up in the object. Sound can trick us into reification but listening is a way of being, regardless of what is heard.

Listening is more subtly active than looking, touching, tasting, or even smelling. Photons percuss against the retina, and molecules strike the olfactory nerves. Liquids saturate the taste buds and waves of air lap against the ear drums. Amongst these air is the roughest touch, but listening does not begin and end in the ears. Distributed throughout the body/mind is a sense of somatic presence, a sensitivity so intimate that the feelings become emotional. Feeling then becomes just the quietest form of listening.

Hearing is primarily a sense of touch. We may be touched at the finely tuned membrane of the eardrum, or at the skin, the skeleton, or the fluid filled spaces of the body. We may be touched by needles or pillows, flitting moments or day-long swells.

Learning to listen

Taking up the violin, not with the aspiration of becoming a great violinist but in order to use it as a tool with which to chart the body-mind, I orientate myself at first by looking. Awkwardly craning my neck, tensing my body like a pointer dog, holding on to an area in front of my head where my fingers dig down and the bow scrapes.

As I learn to release attention from my eyes, though, and allow myself to be buoyed by the sound, I *feel* my position, and then am carried like a boat on a river of sound. As the details of its currents become clear, they wash away my rigidity. Attention dissipates from the point in front of me and my whole body softens and bends in the flow.

Eventually the eyes can close completely to allow a larger sense to saturate a cosmos which is no longer seen 'over there' but which permeates and reverberates through me. What I actually play is immaterial. It cannot be captured by microphones.

Now I do not have to work to create any music but I simply feel it as it passes through fingers and bow. I understand from textbook diagrams that it is my ears that hear but this fact is not clear in the way it is clear that my eyes see. Eyelids and my swivelling neck make the connection between eye and sight much plainer than the connection between ear and hearing. Choice and focus in the visual field are much closer to consciousness. When I listen though, what I hear does not simply enter from outside through my ears. Rather I seem to feel *with* the object, touching all the tingling vibrations of the space and material that constitute my body, the violin, and the reverberating space.

Deep listening is open to much more than just the kind of sound that can be delivered through ear buds. The ears are a gnarled fist. When they open the soft palm of the whole body feels the world. With the ears, I might hear the precise dynamics of intervals and forms, but listening with the body I am situated within a space of resonance; I relate to an architecture of reverberation and timbral mood; I feel rhythms not just over a bar or a phrase but over hours and days and weeks.

Situating myself within sound, it is the place itself which becomes conscious of itself. My body is merely an antenna, a sense organ grown by this place to hear this.

Fading Echoes

I may abandon myself to the raging current or busy myself drily on the banks.

Picking up the violin after months without touching it, I try to remember where I was. Remembering is literally bringing my limbs back into it. My members are brought together again and feel, all at once, as one.

The violin falls back into its slot in my body. The memory of all those past hours comes back to me, but changed. Nothing stays the same. The ease of it returns first. The scars of tension that had begun to crab my muscles have been forgotten, dissolved into the mist of the past. I resolve to keep that relaxation present and not twist myself into tightness at the shoulder, the jaw, the neck, the wrist, the fingers, the face.

The face. If I try to look at my bow against the strings I twist my whole head around and the hard focus of my mind is directed through my eyes. My head is tight and heavy, thinking through every tiny motion, every detail of pressure, position, speed, angle, length. I grit my teeth and flail around on the edge of panic, trying to keep all the variables in mind, trying to keep all these pigeons in my basket. Meanwhile, intonation is a painful screech slipping further and further away, fluttering and sliding through my desperate grasp. There is precious little music in all this, but I soldier on, hoping it will come, trying to nail it down.

Then I remember a different tactic. I close my eyes.

Immediately I can hear better.

But then, because I am moving, because unless I move there is nothing to hear, my feeling and my hearing merge into a larger sense.

Suddenly the speed and position of my bow; its slide and grip against the string; the vibrating line between my left hand and my right; the weight against my collarbone and chest; the round, warm, coloured, complex sound rising from beside my jaw and cheek directly into my left ear and travelling around the room and out into space before returning to my right ear; the feeling of a melody expanding and extending through space, drawing together my body and its surroundings into one incredibly detailed, complex, constantly changing vibration which I can have no hope of ever marshalling or understanding, but to which I can only listen in awe; all this is felt with my whole body and mind.

This is remembering. A bodily listening in which I am an active participant. A dance with the world. Hearing only with wallflower ears seems like timid poverty by comparison.

In the light of day—with my eyes scouring the moment's horizon, looking out for themselves—planning and assessing, in the day I might work out a tune, but it is hard labour. Any satisfaction comes from a sense of control and mastery. But by moonlight, when the hard edges of the world are slightly softened, when my inside and outside are slightly confused, then I begin to be swept up into a dance.

But I keep stumbling and stopping. What is it that makes me falter? What is it that cramps and harries me, draws me again and again into a fight? What is the cause of the wrestling match I stage again and again between myself and the instrument?

The violin becomes a stage for the battle between dancing and trying to play, between listening and trying to listen. The extension and immersiveness of the sound, and the pain in my joints and muscles, are markers of my listening. As I keep moving, I have to work to maintain my concentration. Every time my attention gets twisted and trapped, I have to stoop to untangle it, freeing it to fall back into the flow. I have to do this as many times as it takes, patiently untangling the knots, smilingly wearing out the fighter.

I keep returning to simply feeling the complexity instead of trying to control it. Remembering is the act of bringing the attention back, curbing the hyperactive tendency to improve things. Remembering is continually settling down to just listening, just feeling. Continually and gently prising open the habitually clenched knuckles. Where does that habit come from? Why is it such a fight to learn something I already know? Why am I straining to hear something that is already right here?

Contributors

Lisbeth A. Lipari is an Associate Professor in the Department of Communication at Denison University. Her research and teaching focus on the inter-relationships between language, politics, and ethics. Much of her recent work has involved developing new concepts and vocabulary for understanding listening from cultural, phenomenological, and ethical perspectives.

Diana Corley Schnapp, PhD, is a retired college/university professor who has researched and taught listening and other areas of Speech Communication for more than four decades. She has also written and taught classes in Religion and Bible studies for over forty years. As a Lifetime Member and former Executive Director of the International Listening Association, she remains active in the study of listening from both a theoretical and practical standpoint. She has presented programmes for the International Listening Association and has conducted training in religious, not-for-profit, and business organisations. Her publications include articles in professional journals, text books, trade magazines, and religious magazines.

Daniel Smith is the author of *Muses, Madmen, and Prophets: Hearing Voices and the Borders of Sanity* and the *New York Times* bestseller *Monkey Mind: A Memoir of Anxiety*. His essays and articles have appeared in numerous publications, including *The American Scholar, Granta, n+1, New York,* and *The New York Times Magazine*. He holds the Mary Ellen Donnelly Critchlow Endowed Chair in English at The College of New Rochelle.

Nicola Triscott is a cultural producer and writer, specializing in the intersections between art, science, technology and society. She is the founder and Director of The Arts Catalyst, one of the UK's most distinctive arts organizations, distinguished by ambitious artists' commissions that engage with science. She lectures and publishes internationally, and has curated many exhibitions and events. In 2007, she was awarded a Clore Leadership Fellowship. From 2007–9 she was Visiting Researcher at London South Bank University. She is the founder of Catalyst Rwanda, working with vulnerable young people and emerging artists in Rwanda.

Jean de Dieu Basabose is the co-founder and executive Director of Shalom Educating for Peace and a committed Rwandan Peacebuilder. He holds a Masters degree in Conflict Resolution and Peace Studies from the University of Kwazulu-Natal. Since 2003, he has been making efforts to educate communities for peace and build skills for nonviolent conflict resolution. He believes that education is a powerful weapon to transform human society from militaristic to humanistic and nonviolent ways of dealing with conflicts. He is undertaking doctoral research focusing on anti-corruption education as a way of building positive peace in Rwanda.

Polly Nash has been working in film and television since 1988 when she started out with Steel Bank Film Co-op in Sheffield. After graduating from the Royal College of Art in 1994, she worked as Production Manager and Assistant Director on television documentary and drama, contributing to strands such as *Dispatches, Critical Eye* and *Cutting Edge*. In 1997 she started working as a producer with the documentary company Spectacle. As an independent producer she has produced films with artists such as Steve McQueen (*Stage*), Rachel Davies (*Gold*) and Jocelyn Cammack (*The Bone Orchestra*). Her most recent film *Outside The Law: Stories from Guantánamo* is a 75min feature, made with journalist Andy Worthington.

Kenneth Avery learned music, piano and guitar from an early age, and graduated from the University of Sydney in 1981, having studied Hebrew, Arabic and Persian. He was introduced to the Sufi path in his student days, and later gained a PhD from the University of Melbourne. His thesis was published by Routledge in 2004 as *A Psychology of Early Sufi sama: Listening and Altered States.* He has also published (with Ali Alizadeh) *Fifty Poems of Attar,* translations from the great 12th century Sufi poet. He works as a music teacher in rural Victoria, Australia.

Seth Ayyaz Bhunnoo is a composer-performer working with sound-based composition, live electronics, and Islamic instrumental music traditions. He is a PhD (Composition) candidate at City University London and is also trained in Neurosciences, psychology and medicine. He has published in *Organised Sound* and *The Wire* and presented at international conferences including the World Forum for Acoustic Ecology in Finland, and Music and the Body in Hong Kong. His focus is on listening and investigating what a sonic body can do. He builds ecologies for specific performances, and improvises/composes with other listening machines, human or otherwise.

Niall Atkinson is the Neubauer Family Assistant Professor of Art History at the University of Chicago. His research has focused on urban experience in late medieval and Renaissance Italy, which has led to an investigation of how the soundscape of early modern Florence was a crucial factor in binding urban communities to the physical spaces of the built environment. Currently he has expanded this investigation to a more comprehensive study of architecture's relationship to the body's entire sensorial matrix as a way of shedding new light on the urban condition of Renaissance Italy.

Ansuman Biswas was born in India and is now based in the UK. His practice incorporates, and often hybridizes, music, film, live art, installation, architecture, writing and theatre. This inter-disciplinarity is founded on a core training in contemplation which has informed his commitment to the primacy of listening and the fluidity of identity. He is also a Trustee of Arts Catalyst, working with artists and scientists; and Studio Upstairs, working with the arts and mental health.
www.ansuman.co.uk